ESSENTIAL CHEMISTRY

EARTH CHEMISTRY

ESSENTIAL CHEMISTRY

Atoms, Molecules, and Compounds

Chemical Reactions

Metals

The Periodic Table

States of Matter

Acids and Bases

Biochemistry

Carbon Chemistry

Chemical Bonds

Earth Chemistry

ESSENTIAL CHEMISTRY

EARTH CHEMISTRY

ALLAN B. COBB

CHELSEA HOUSE
PUBLISHERS
An imprint of Infobase Publishing

EARTH CHEMISTRY

Chelsea House
An imprint of Infobase Publishing
132 West 31st Street
New York NY 10001

Library of Congress Cataloging-in-Publication Data

Cobb, Allan B.
  Earth chemistry / Allan B. Cobb.
    p. cm. — (Essential chemistry)
  Includes bibliographical references.
  ISBN 978-0-7910-9677-2 (hardcover)
  1. Environmental chemistry. I. Title.

  TD193.C63 2008
  551.9—dc22   2007051317

Chelsea House books are available at special discounts when purchased in bulk quantities for businesses, associations, institutions, or sales promotions. Please call our Special Sales Department in New York at (212) 967-8800 or (800) 322-8755.

You can find Chelsea House on the World Wide Web at http://www.chelseahouse.com

Text design by Erik Lindstrom
Cover design by Ben Peterson

Printed in the United States of America

Bang NMSG 10 9 8 7 6 5 4 3 2 1

This book is printed on acid-free paper.

All links and Web addresses were checked and verified to be correct at the time of publication. Because of the dynamic nature of the Web, some addresses and links may have changed since publication and may no longer be valid.

CONTENTS

1 **Earth** 1

2 **The Atmosphere** 15

3 **Chemical Processes in the Atmosphere** 29

4 **The Hydrosphere** 42

5 **Chemical and Physical Processes in the Hydrosphere** 55

6 **The Lithosphere** 68

7 **Chemical Processes in the Lithosphere** 80

8 **Biosphere** 93

Periodic Table of the Elements 106

Electron Configurations 108

Table of Atomic Masses 110

Glossary 112

Bibliography 120

Further Reading 121

Photo Credits 122

Index 123

About the Author 130

Earth

In scientific terms, a **system** is any set of interactions that can be separated from the rest of the universe for the purposes of study, observation, and measurement. Therefore, a system is something in which the various parts fit together and seamlessly work in harmony. Earth has four major systems that work together. These systems are identified as the hydrosphere, the atmosphere, the lithosphere, and the biosphere.

Of all the planets in our solar system, Earth stands out because of the presence of water. When viewed from space, the first notable feature about our planet is its blue color. This color comes from the oceans of water that cover more than 70% of its surface. No other planet in our solar system has liquid water on its surface.

The next feature that stands out is the scattered clouds that move about. These clouds indicate that Earth is surrounded by an atmosphere containing water vapor. Below the clouds, the land surfaces look interesting because they show signs of geologic processes that form mountains. Finally, there is a huge coral reef—the Great Barrier Reef—off the Australian continent. This is unique because living organisms built it. These characteristics show from afar that Earth has a hydrosphere, atmosphere, lithosphere, and biosphere.

The **hydrosphere** includes all water on Earth. As mentioned earlier, the abundance of water on Earth is a unique feature that clearly distinguishes Earth from other planets in the solar system. Liquid water is not found anywhere else in the solar system. The hydrosphere exists because conditions on Earth are just right. These conditions include Earth's chemical composition, atmosphere, and distance from the Sun. Water on Earth exists in all three states of matter—solid (ice), liquid (water), and gas (water vapor). Water has the ability to hold heat, so it buffers Earth's surface from large temperature changes.

The **atmosphere** is the blanket of gases that surrounds Earth. This blanket constitutes the transition between Earth's surface and the vacuum of space. The atmosphere is a mixture of gases composed primarily of nitrogen, oxygen, carbon dioxide, and water vapor. The atmosphere extends to about 300 miles (500 kilometers) above the surface of the Earth. It is divided into levels, or layers, each with its own characteristics. The lowest level, the troposphere, maintains conditions suitable for life. The next level above, the stratosphere, contains the **ozone** layer that protects life on Earth by filtering harmful ultraviolet radiation from the Sun.

Certain gases in the atmosphere help maintain the warm temperatures found on Earth. These gases trap thermal energy emitted from Earth's surface, preventing it from escaping into space and thereby increasing global temperatures. This action helps to maintain an average temperature on Earth well above the freezing point of water.

The **lithosphere** is the rocky surface of Earth that includes the regions of dry land and ocean floors. Ninety-four percent of the lithosphere is composed of the elements oxygen, iron, silicon, and magnesium. The lithosphere is very dynamic. Energy from Earth's interior causes the planet's surface to be in a constant state of motion. This motion gives rise to the movement of the continents. These movements are responsible for building mountains and recycling materials between Earth's surface and its interior.

The **biosphere** is the living part of Earth. It is the sum total of all living things on the planet. The biosphere is an integrated system whose many components fit together in complex ways. The biosphere works in conjunction with the other major Earth systems. Chemical elements and compounds essential to life circulate through each of the systems. Carbon is part of all living organisms, and it cycles through all four Earth systems. This cycling of carbon is called a biogeochemical cycle because it is driven by biological, geological, and chemical processes. Water is another important biogeochemical cycle. The cycling of water among the Earth systems is called the hydrologic cycle or, more commonly, the water cycle.

THE WATER CYCLE

The **water cycle** is a biogeochemical cycle that moves water from the oceans, rivers, streams, lakes, and so on, through the atmosphere, and back to Earth's surface. A molecule of water consists of two hydrogen atoms bonded to an oxygen atom. The bonding between the hydrogen and oxygen gives water many unique properties. Because water exists on Earth as a solid, liquid, and gas, all three forms of matter are part of the water cycle. The water cycle depends on five separate processes—evaporation, condensation, precipitation, runoff, and infiltration.

The oceans are the major reservoir of water on Earth. The world's oceans cover nearly 71% of the planet's surface. When the Sun shines on the oceans, the surface water warms, and some of it evaporates. **Evaporation** is the process by which matter changes from a liquid state to a gaseous state. In this case, liquid water changes into water vapor, which is a gas. Energy from the Sun causes evaporation because it raises the temperature of liquid water. As water molecules at the surface of a body of water heat up, the molecules gain energy and are released into the atmosphere as a gas. This process also warms the air above the water. Warm air rises into the atmosphere, carrying the water vapor with it.

As the mixture of warm air and water vapor rises, it expands and cools. Warm air can hold more water than can cool air. As the air cools, it can no longer hold as much water vapor, so the water vapor condenses. **Condensation** is the process by which a gas changes to a liquid. The water vapor in the atmosphere condenses to form clouds. In the atmosphere, water changes back and forth between states as the air temperature fluctuates. This explains why some days are cloudy and some are not. When moist air cools enough, water vapor condenses to form clouds. If air temperature rises again, cloud droplets evaporate to form water vapor, and the clouds disappear.

As clouds form, winds move them across Earth's surface, spreading out the water vapor. Sometimes, so much water condenses that the clouds can no longer hold the moisture. When this happens, the excess water falls back to Earth's surface as precipitation. **Precipitation** is water that falls from clouds in the form of rain, snow, sleet, or hail. Precipitation either falls into the ocean or onto land. Water that falls into the ocean is ready to evaporate again and continue its role in the water cycle.

When water falls on land, runoff and infiltration take place simultaneously. **Infiltration** occurs when precipitation seeps into the ground. The amount of water that seeps into the ground depends on soil conditions. **Permeability** is the measure of how easily a fluid—a gas or a liquid—moves through a material. Therefore, the more permeable a soil is, the easier it is for water to seep into it. Sometimes, the rate of precipitation is greater than the amount of water that can infiltrate the ground. When this occurs, the excess water becomes **runoff**. Runoff flows across

Earth's surface into rivers and then into lakes or oceans. Some water that seeps into the ground becomes **groundwater**. Groundwater usually moves much more slowly than the surface water in rivers and streams. Groundwater eventually reaches the surface at springs or in water wells.

Water at the Earth's surface may also evaporate. When this happens, the water vapor re-enters the water cycle and eventually falls as precipitation. Plants use some of the water that infiltrates the ground. Plants take in water through their roots and lose it as water vapor through leaves. This process by which plants release water vapor is called **transpiration**.

The processes of the hydrologic cycle continue to move water from the oceans to the atmosphere and back to the Earth's surface. It is estimated that 100 million billion gallons a year are cycled through this process.

TYPES OF ROCKS

As described earlier, the hard outer portion of Earth is called the lithosphere. The upper rocky portion of the lithosphere is called the crust. The rocks that make up the crust are composed primarily of **minerals**. A mineral is a nonliving crystalline material that occurs in nature and has a definite chemical composition. Rocks may be made up of two or more different minerals or can be composed of a single mineral. More than 3,500 minerals have been identified. Fewer than 20 minerals, however, compose more than 95% of the rocks that make up Earth's crust. Rocks are classified by the way they are formed. The three basic types of rocks are igneous, sedimentary, and metamorphic.

Igneous Rock

Igneous rocks are formed from hot, molten minerals that come from Earth's interior. These rocks are formed from magma that cools beneath Earth's surface and also from lava that cools at Earth's surface. Rocks that form beneath Earth's surface are called

intrusive igneous rocks. Rocks that form at Earth's surface are called **extrusive igneous rocks**.

Intrusive igneous rocks form from molten material that cools very slowly. These rocks usually contain larger mineral **crystals** than do igneous rocks which form from material that cools more quickly. Magma can take thousands of years to cool. Lava, which reaches Earth's surface from volcanoes or fissures in the crust, cools much more quickly. Extrusive igneous rocks often have small crystals. Basalt, which is formed from lava, is the most common type of igneous rock. Basalt is found on the ocean floor and covers a large portion of Earth's surface.

Sedimentary Rock

Existing rock fragments or shells become cemented, compacted, and hardened to form **sedimentary rocks**. Once rocks are exposed at Earth's surface, they are weathered or broken down, and the fragments are transported and deposited as **sediments**. Over time, deep-lying sediments become cemented together, compacted, and hardened by the weight and pressure exerted on them by the sediments above them. Eventually, the sediments are **lithified** and become sedimentary rock. Sediments that come together in this way are known as **clastic** sediments.

Some sedimentary rocks form by a chemical process called **precipitation**. During this process, calcium carbonate precipitates out of seawater and helps produce the shells of tiny marine organisms. After these organisms eventually die and are buried, the calcium carbonate becomes lithified to form limestone. Most limestone is a **biochemical** product of calcium carbonate created by the remains of dead creatures.

Metamorphic Rock

Metamorphic rock is formed as a result of great pressure and temperature being applied to existing rock, thereby converting it into a new, distinct type of rock. All types of rocks can be changed into metamorphic rocks. Sedimentary rocks can become metamorphic rocks if the weight of rock materials above them exerts enough heat and pressure to change their structure. A given type of rock can only change into a given type of metamorphic rock. The sedimentary rock limestone, for example, always becomes marble when metamorphosed. Shale, another sedimentary rock, changes into slate.

THE ROCK CYCLE

The **rock cycle** is a series of changes that rocks undergo. It is one of the fundamental concepts of geology. Igneous rock can change into sedimentary rock or into metamorphic rock. Sedimentary rock can change into metamorphic rock or into igneous rock. Metamorphic rock can change into igneous or sedimentary rock. Each basic rock type can change into another type of rock under the right conditions.

EROSION AND DEPOSITION

Earth's surface is constantly being changed by the processes of weathering and erosion. **Weathering** is the physical and chemical breaking down of rock at Earth's surface by wind, water, ice, chemicals, plant roots, and burrowing animals. **Erosion** is the removal of weathered rock materials and the transport of those materials from one place to another. This powerful force can shape landscapes and carve deep valleys. Erosion removes sediments from the land, especially from riverbanks and shorelines, and transports the eroded material downslope.

The major agents of erosion are wind, moving water, and moving ice. These agents are powered by gravity. The process of erosion stops when the transporting agent slows down or stops moving and the particles the agent carries are dropped onto a surface. This process is called **deposition**. Erosion and deposition are natural processes. These two processes always work together, because materials eroded from one location must be deposited somewhere else.

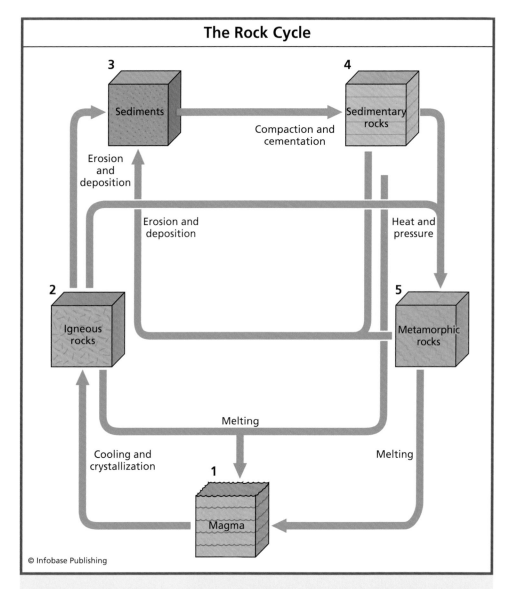

The Rock Cycle

3 Sediments

4 Sedimentary rocks

Compaction and cementation

Erosion and deposition

Erosion and deposition

Heat and pressure

2 Igneous rocks

5 Metamorphic rocks

Melting

Cooling and crystallization

Melting

1 Magma

© Infobase Publishing

Figure 1.1   The rock cycle explains how the three rock types are related to each other and how different natural processes change a rock from one type to another.

Some materials are more easily eroded than others. Flowing water or blowing wind easily pick up and carry soft material, such as soil or sand. Other materials, such as rock, are more difficult to erode. However, even the hardest rocks will eventually be weathered and eroded. The Grand Canyon is an example of the relentless power of erosion.

THE GRAND CANYON

The Grand Canyon is located in Arizona. It is a deep gorge carved by the Colorado River. The Grand Canyon is 277 miles (446 km) long, 4 to 18 miles (6 to 30 km) wide, and up to 1 mile (1.6 km) deep. It has taken the Colorado River over 6 million years to carve through the rocks. The rocks exposed in the canyon walls represent more than 2 billion years of Earth's history. Most of the Grand Canyon is located in Grand Canyon National Park.

Figure 1.2   The Grand Canyon is a steep-sided gorge carved by the Colorado River.

EARTH'S STRUCTURE—CORE, MANTLE, CRUST

Earth's structure consists of three main layers: the core, the mantle, and the crust. Scientists have not been able to directly observe Earth's interior, so they must collect indirect data to tell them about this region. Scientists have learned much about the interior of Earth by studying seismic waves. Seismic waves are energy waves that travel through Earth. Scientists measure these waves at various locations around the planet. By measuring the nature of the waves and changes in velocity and direction, scientists have learned about the properties of Earth's interior.

The innermost part of Earth is the **core**, a dense sphere made up of the elements iron and nickel. It is divided into two parts. The inner core, at the very center of the Earth, is a solid ball 780 miles (1,220 km) in diameter. Even at temperatures greater than 10,000°F (5,500°C), the inner core remains solid because of the extreme pressure around it. The outer core, where pressure is lower, is always molten. The temperature of the outer core reaches 6700°F (3,700°C). The outer core is about 1,370 miles (2,200 km) thick. Because the Earth rotates on its axis, the outer core spins around the inner core, creating a magnetic field around the planet.

The layer above the outer core is the **mantle**. It begins about 6 miles (10 km) below the oceanic crust and about 19 miles (30 km) below the continental crust. The mantle is divided into the inner mantle and the outer mantle. Together, both parts are about 1,800 miles (2,900 km) thick and make up nearly 80% of the Earth's total volume. The material in the mantle is hot enough that the rocks act like a very thick plastic. This enables the mantle to move, or "flow," very slowly.

The **crust** is above the mantle and is Earth's hard outer shell, the surface on which we live. The crust is by far the thinnest of Earth's three layers. The crust seems to "float" on the denser upper portion of the mantle. In fact, the crust and the upper mantle together make up the hard outer shell of Earth known as the lithosphere.

The crust is made up of solid material, but the composition of the crust varies from place to place. In general, there are two types

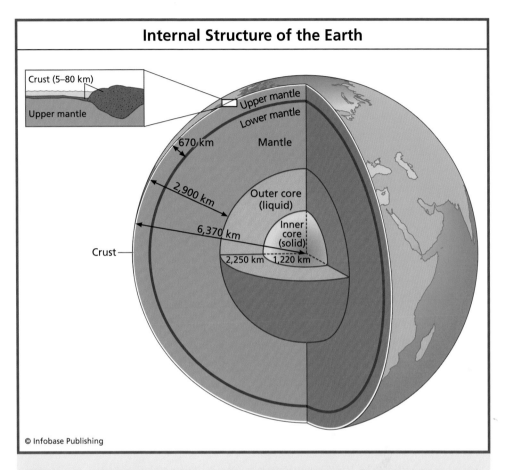

Internal Structure of the Earth

Crust (5–80 km)

Upper mantle

Upper mantle

Lower mantle

670 km

Mantle

2,900 km

Outer core
(liquid)

6,370 km

Inner
core
(solid)

Crust

2,250 km   1,220 km

© Infobase Publishing

Figure 1.2   This diagram shows a section of the Earth removed to reveal the internal structure of the planet.

of crust—oceanic crust and continental crust. Oceanic crust is about 4 to 7 miles (6 to 11 km) thick and consists mainly of basalt. The continental crust is thicker than the oceanic crust, about 19 miles (30 km) thick, and is made up mainly of granite.

PLATE TECTONICS

The theory of **plate tectonics** revolutionized the field of geology. The theory was developed in the 1960s and 1970s based on studies about the ocean floor, Earth's magnetism, chains of volcanoes, zones of frequent earthquake activity, Earth's interior, and the distribution of fossils. All of these factors provided clues that led to the development of the theory.

According to the theory of plate tectonics, Earth's lithosphere is broken into seven large, rigid pieces and several smaller pieces. These pieces of the lithosphere are called tectonic plates. The major tectonic plates are the African, North American, South American, Eurasian, Australian, Antarctic, and Pacific plates. The plates are all moving slowly across Earth's surface in different directions and at different speeds. The speed of these plates ranges from about three-quarters of an inch to 4 inches (2 centimeters to 10 centimeters) per year. Each plate is moving in relation to other plates. In different places across Earth's surface, the plates crash together, pull apart, or grind against each other. The region where two plates meet is called a plate boundary. What happens at a plate boundary depends on how the two plates are moving relative to each other.

A region where two plates collide is called a **convergent boundary**. Because plates only move a few centimeters each year, these collisions happen very slowly. However, even at very slow speeds, plate collisions generate incredible force. For example, along a boundary where an oceanic plate collides with a continental plate, the denser oceanic plate is pushed under the continental plate, while the edge of the continental plate is pushed up, creating a huge mountain range. A trench forms in the region where the oceanic plate is thrust beneath the continental plate. Rock along the boundaries of both plates breaks and slips, causing earthquakes. As the edge of the oceanic plate plunges into the upper mantle, some of the rock melts. This molten rock rises up as magma through the continental plate. This action causes earthquakes and, where the molten rock reaches the surface, forms a volcano.

A region where plates are moving apart is called a **divergent boundary**. When the lithosphere moves apart, it typically breaks along parallel **faults**, or cracks in Earth's crust. As the plates pull apart, huge blocks of crust between the faults sink. The sinking of

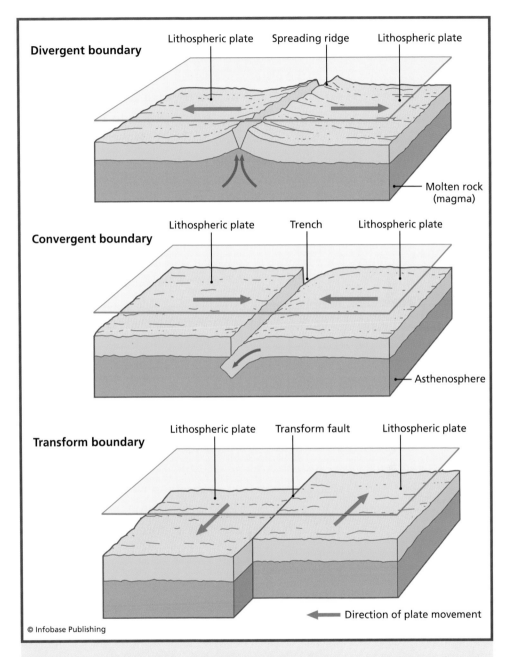

Figure 1.3   The tectonic movement of plates results in three types of plate boundaries. Which type depends on the relative motion of the plates.

the blocks forms a central valley called a **rift**. Magma seeps upward to fill the cracks, forming new crust. Earthquakes are common along the faults as the plates pull apart. In places where the magma reaches the surface, volcanoes form. When a divergent boundary crosses land, it forms a rift valley that may be 18 to 31 miles (30 to 50 km) wide. When a divergent boundary crosses the ocean floor, the rift valley formed is narrow, up to about 0.5 mile (1 km) wide. A rift valley formed on the ocean floor is called a **mid-oceanic ridge**. Networks of mid-oceanic ridges run through the centers of Earth's major ocean basins.

A region where plates slide past each other is called a **transform boundary**. The presence of transform boundaries are indicated in some places by the existence of linear valleys along the boundary. The sliding motion between the plates causes a high number of earthquakes. The San Andreas Fault in California is a well-known transform boundary.

ANALYZING EARTH SYSTEMS

This introduction to Earth and Earth systems is meant to provide a background for understanding Earth chemistry. Each of the major characteristics of Earth—atmosphere, hydrosphere, lithosphere, and biosphere—will be covered in further detail. Each of these will be covered as a system, and their connections with one another will be described. One point that is emphasized throughout this book is that because the Earth systems are interconnected, an event in one system will affect other systems. In addition, these components of Earth provide the necessities for life, and set Earth apart from the other planets in the solar system.

The Atmosphere

The atmosphere is all around us. It is the transparent envelope of gases that surrounds Earth. We depend on the atmosphere for the air we breathe. The atmosphere is often taken for granted because we do not see it, feel it, or taste it. However, the atmosphere is present and it has a profound affect on Earth and all of its living organisms.

COMPOSITION

The atmosphere is made up of a solution of different gases which, taken together, make up air. Three gases make up 99.96% of the gases in dry air by volume. These gases are nitrogen (N_2, 78.1%), oxygen (O_2, 20.9%), and argon (Ar, 0.93%). Other gases in the atmosphere include water vapor (H_2O), carbon dioxide (CO_2), methane (CH_4), ozone (O_3), and nitrous oxide (NO_2).

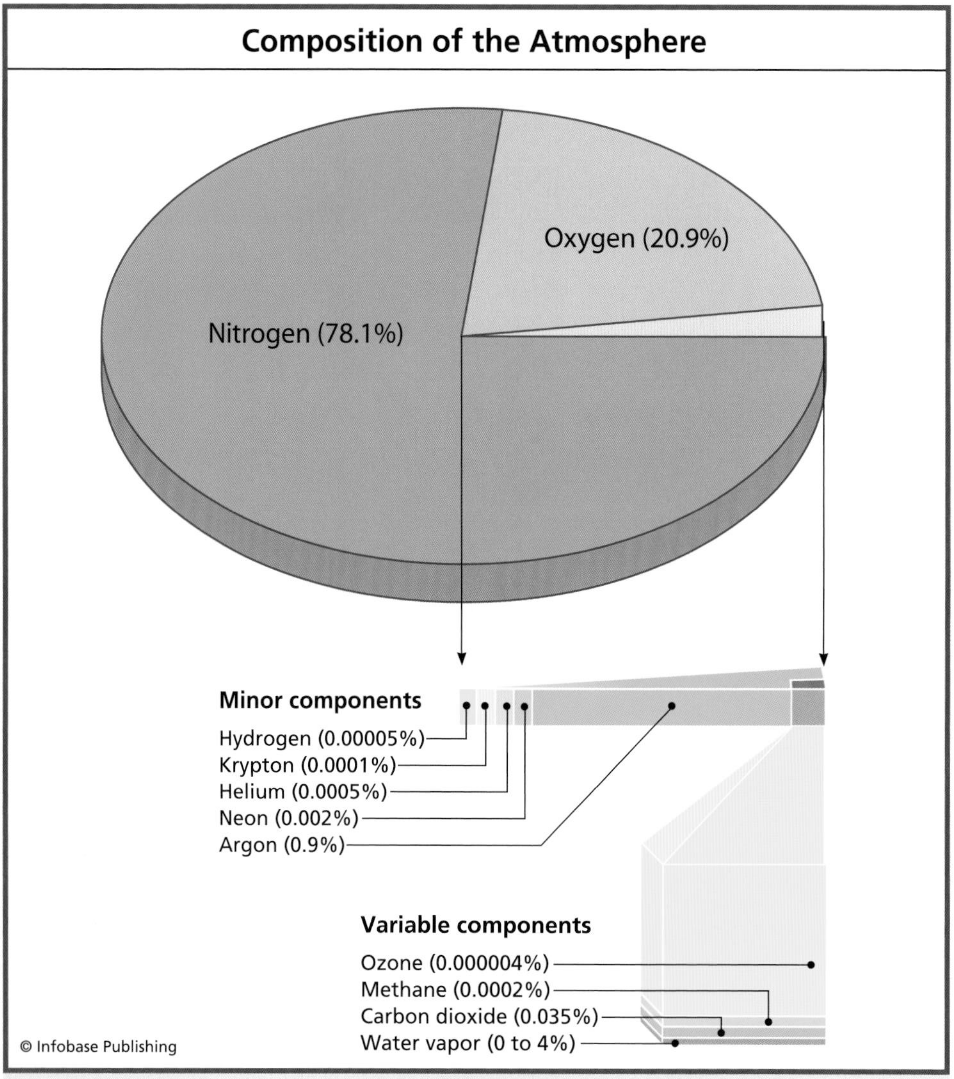

Composition of the Atmosphere

Oxygen (20.9%)

Nitrogen (78.1%)

Minor components

Hydrogen (0.00005%)
Krypton (0.0001%)
Helium (0.0005%)
Neon (0.002%)
Argon (0.9%)

Variable components

Ozone (0.000004%)
Methane (0.0002%)
Carbon dioxide (0.035%)
Water vapor (0 to 4%)

© Infobase Publishing

Figure 2.1   The atmosphere of Earth is composed mainly of nitrogen and oxygen. All the other gases in the atmosphere make up the remainder.

Water Vapor

The amount of water vapor in the air varies greatly from day to day and from place to place. High in the atmosphere, water vapor is absent. One of the major factors that control the amount of water vapor in the atmosphere is temperature. Warm air can hold more water vapor than cold air. The amount of water vapor in the atmosphere is called **humidity**. Humidity that is measured by the amount of water in a given volume of air is called absolute humidity. Absolute humidity is usually expressed as kilograms of water per cubic meter of air. Absolute humidity is seldom used because it can change with temperature and pressure of the air. Water vapor in the atmosphere is usually expressed as **relative humidity**. Relative humidity is the ratio of the amount of water vapor in a parcel of air to the amount that the air could hold if saturated at the same temperature. Relative humidity is expressed as a percentage.

Carbon Dioxide

As of January 2007, the carbon dioxide content of the atmosphere is 383 parts per million (ppm). The concentration of carbon dioxide has been rising since about 1850, when the carbon dioxide level was about 280 ppm. The increase of more than 100 ppm is due mainly to the burning of fossil fuels. When fossil fuels are burned, carbon dioxide is released into the atmosphere. Carbon dioxide is called a **greenhouse gas** because it contributes to the **greenhouse effect**.

When Earth's surface absorbs energy from the Sun, some of that energy is changed into thermal energy. Thermal energy is the sum of the kinetic energy of molecular movement in matter. This energy is radiated back into the atmosphere as heat in the form of infrared waves. Greenhouse gases such as carbon dioxide and methane have the ability to absorb infrared energy and prevent it from escaping into space. The greenhouse effect will be discussed in greater detail in the next chapter.

Aerosols

Tiny particles of liquids and solids are also present in the atmosphere. One such particle you are familiar with is dust. Dust particles are large enough that they can settle out of air. Particles of solids and liquids less than one-thousandth of a millimeter that are suspended in the atmosphere are called **aerosols**. Aerosols include water droplets that make up clouds; smoke from fires; particles of sea salt; and pollutants such as sulfur dioxide (SO_2). Some aerosols have an effect on climate and their role will be covered in the next chapter.

THICKNESS AND PRESSURE OF THE ATMOSPHERE

Earth's atmosphere has mass. The estimated mass of the atmosphere is about 5×10^{18} kg. The actual height of the atmosphere is difficult to measure because there is no sharp division between "empty" space and the upper regions of the atmosphere. Even 62 miles (100 km) above the Earth's surface, some atmospheric gases are present. However, these gas molecules are very widely separated. Gravity exerts a force on the gases in the atmosphere, pulling them toward Earth's surface. This gravitational force causes air pressure.

Air is a fluid, like water. As you probably know, the deeper you descend into a body of water, the greater the pressure the water exerts on your body. This increase in pressure is produced by the weight of the water above pressing on you from all directions. The same phenomenon occurs in the air. Think of the atmosphere as an "ocean" of air. The closer you are to the bottom of this ocean, the greater the pressure it exerts.

At sea level, average atmospheric pressure is about 760 mm of mercury (called torr, a unit of pressure), 101.3 kilopascals, or 14.7 pounds per square inch. Each of these values is the same; they are just expressed in different units. Weather forecasters usually report air pressure as the barometric pressure, which is measured with an instrument called a barometer. The average barometric pressure at sea level is 29.92 inches (760 millimeters) of mercury.

A mercury barometer consists of a vertical glass tube sealed at one end and filled with mercury. The open end of the tube is inserted into a reservoir of mercury. Pressure from the atmosphere pushes on the mercury, which then pushes the mercury in the sealed tube higher or lower depending on the barometric pressure. At average barometric pressure, the atmosphere supports a column of mercury 29.92 inches (76 centimeters) high in the tube. As air pressure increases, more force is exerted on the mercury in the reservoir and mercury is pushed higher into the tube. As air pressure decreases, less force is exerted on the mercury reservoir and the level in the tube falls. These changes in barometric pressure

COOKING AT HIGH ALTITUDE

Water boils at 100°C (212°F). This is only true at sea level and at average air pressure. Actually, the boiling point of water, or any liquid, is the temperature at which the vapor pressure of the liquid is equal to the atmospheric pressure. As air pressure decreases, the temperature at which the vapor pressure is equal to the atmospheric pressure also decreases. At an elevation of 300 meters, the boiling point of water is 210°F (98.7°C). At 3000 meters in elevation, the boiling point of water is 192°F (88.9°C).

This change in the boiling point of water means that at the reduced air pressure found at higher elevations, it takes longer to cook foods by boiling. Potatoes, pasta, and rice all take longer to cook because the temperature of the boiling water is lower. Many packaged foods list extended cooking times for higher altitudes. One way around this problem is to use a pressure cooker. Pressure cookers are partially sealed to increase the pressure inside as liquids are heated. This increase in pressure means that water boils at a temperature higher than 100°C so foods cook faster.

are used to predict weather. The reasons for changes in barometric pressure will be explained later in this chapter.

ATMOSPHERIC LAYERS

Earth's atmosphere is divided into five layers—troposphere, stratosphere, mesosphere, thermosphere, and exosphere. Each of these layers has distinct characteristics.

The **troposphere** is the layer closest to Earth's surface. It extends up to 11 miles (18 km) at the equator and about 4.2 miles (7 km) at the poles. The troposphere is a very active layer. Solar heating causes winds and extensive mixing in the troposphere. Most weather takes place in this layer. In the troposphere, the temperature of dry air decreases with height at an average rate of 43.7°F (6.5°C) for every 0.6 mile (1 km) increase in height. As the air rises, cooling from the expanding gases causes the decrease in temperature.

The **stratosphere** is the layer that lies above the troposphere. It extends from the top of the troposphere to a height of about 32 miles (50 km). In the stratosphere, temperature increases as altitude increases. This change occurs because the layer is heated from above by absorption of ultraviolet radiation from the Sun. At the top of the stratosphere, the temperature is slightly below the freezing point of water. The heating in the stratosphere is caused by the presence of a layer of ozone (O_3). The ozone absorbs ultraviolet radiation and warms the surrounding atmosphere. This action also prevents much of the Sun's ultraviolet radiation from reaching Earth's surface.

The **mesosphere** is the layer above the stratosphere. The mesosphere extends from the top of the stratosphere to a height of about 53 miles (85 km). In the mesosphere, temperature decreases as altitude increases. At the top of the mesosphere, the temperature is about −148°F (−100°C). In addition to gases, the mesosphere also has a high concentration of iron and other metal atoms because meteors burn up in this layer.

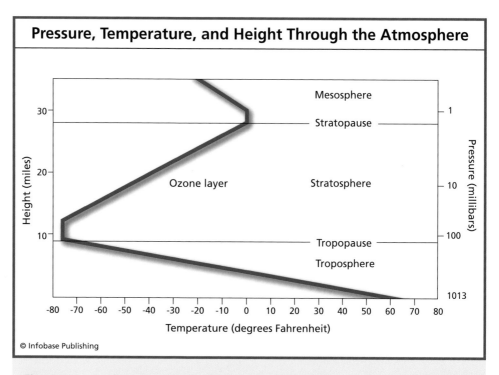

Pressure, Temperature, and Height Through the Atmosphere

Mesosphere

Stratopause

Ozone layer

Stratosphere

Tropopause

Troposphere

Height (miles)

Pressure (millibars)

Temperature (degrees Fahrenheit)

© Infobase Publishing

Figure 2.2   In the troposphere, the temperature decreases with altitude because the warming is caused by heat radiating from the Earth's surface. In the stratosphere, the temperature increases because ozone absorbs solar radiation and warms the atmosphere.

The thermosphere is the layer above the mesosphere. It extends outward to between 310 and 620 miles (500 and 1,000 km). The temperature of the thermosphere reaches 4,532°F (2,500°C) during the daytime. The temperature is so high in the thermosphere because the few gas molecules present receive a tremendous amount of energy from the Sun. One layer of the thermosphere is called the ionosphere. The ionosphere has free electrons that exist for only a short period of time. They form as a result of energy from the Sun, but they quickly lose energy because they are unstable. This process creates a continual stream of ionic particles. These free electrons are sufficient to reflect radio waves. Radio waves bounce off the "surface" of the ionosphere and return to Earth's surface, thus allowing radios to work.

The outermost layer of the Earth's atmosphere is the **exosphere**. The exosphere extends outward more than 6,214 miles (10,000 km). In the exosphere, the pressure is very low and some of the gas particles escape the atmosphere into space. Most satellites orbit within this layer of the atmosphere. The temperature of the exosphere is very high due to the fact that there are very few gas molecules present to absorb energy from the Sun.

ORIGIN AND EVOLUTION OF THE ATMOSPHERE

Scientists have pieced together evidence to explain how the early atmosphere formed. According to their findings, the atmosphere on Earth has undergone three distinct composition changes. Scientists sometimes refer to our current atmosphere as the third atmosphere.

Earth's first atmosphere was likely made up of helium and hydrogen. Heat from the molten surface and solar energy from the Sun likely forced this atmosphere from the planet as quickly as it formed. About 4.5 billion years ago, Earth's surface finally cooled enough to allow a crust to form. The surface was active with volcanoes, which likely released water in the form of steam, carbon dioxide, ammonia, and hydrogen. These gases helped create the second atmosphere. Over time, these gases continued to build up. Eventually, the second atmosphere had a much larger gas volume than today's atmosphere, so it exerted a greater pressure. Because of the high concentration of greenhouse gases, the planet was very warm, even though the Sun's solar output was likely less than it is today.

About 3.3 billion years ago, *cyanobacteria*, one of the earliest forms of life, became numerous. Cyanobacteria are the most primitive photosynthetic organisms. The cyanobacteria used the Sun's energy to convert carbon dioxide and water into food in the form of hydrocarbons. The byproduct of this reaction is oxygen.

The actions of the cyanobacteria began adding oxygen to the atmosphere for the first time. Much of this oxygen did not remain long in the early atmosphere. It quickly combined with metals to form oxides (such as iron to form iron oxide) and with ammonia in the atmosphere to form nitrogen and water. As more plants appeared, the plants converted the carbon dioxide in the atmosphere into oxygen while producing **biomass**. Oxygen levels began increasing in the atmosphere as the rate of production from photosynthesis exceeded the rate of oxidation.

The high levels of carbon dioxide in the atmosphere were reduced through several processes. First, plants converted some of the carbon dioxide into biomass. Some of the biomass was buried and converted into fossil fuels such as coal, petroleum, and natural gas. The oceans absorbed some of the carbon dioxide. Some of this dissolved carbon dioxide underwent chemical reactions and precipitated out of seawater as calcium carbonate. Some organisms evolved and used the calcium carbonate in the water to make shells. The shells of these deceased organisms and precipitated calcium carbonate hardened and turned into limestone.

Ammonia in the atmosphere reacted with oxygen to release nitrogen gas. Some bacteria evolved that were able to use ammonia as an energy source. They also released nitrogen. Most of the ammonia in the atmosphere decomposed through **photolysis**. Photolysis is a chemical reaction in which photons (bundles of energy) from light break down chemical compounds.

These changes in the atmosphere not only affected the oceans and land surfaces, but they also affected the biosphere. As living organisms first evolved, they lived in an **anoxic** environment, which is an environement that lacks oxygen. As the atmosphere became oxic, or oxygen containing, these early organisms could no longer survive just anywhere. The oxygen in the atmosphere was toxic to these organisms because it interfered with their metabolism. These organisms became restricted only to certain extreme environments where oxygen was not present (such as deep in the oceans). New organisms evolved that could use oxygen. These changes in the atmosphere caused major changes in the makeup of life on Earth.

All of these processes slowly worked together to create what scientists call the third atmosphere. The third atmosphere is dominated by nitrogen and oxygen. The amounts of these two elements have varied up and down, sometimes greatly. By about 200 to 250 million years ago, the oxygen concentration was up to about 35% in the atmosphere. At other times, the atmosphere contained little free oxygen.

The presence of oxygen in the early atmosphere led to the development of ozone in the stratosphere. As oxygen spread into the stratosphere, some of it collected in a region now known as the ozone layer. In this part of the stratosphere, diatomic oxygen molecules react with ultraviolet radiation to form ozone (O_3). The ozone provided a shield that protected Earth's surface by absorbing much of the ultraviolet radiation from the Sun. This protection affected the evolution of land plants and animals. During times of high oxygen concentrations, animals flourished and many new species evolved. During times of little or no oxygen, mass extinctions took place. Two main oxygen consumers—chemical weathering and animal respiration—control the amount of oxygen in the atmosphere. The current concentrations of nitrogen and oxygen have been relatively stable for millions of years. However, in recent years, another change to the atmosphere has been taking place. The burning of fossil fuels has been causing the release of carbon dioxide into the atmosphere. This has resulted in an increase in the concentration of carbon dioxide in the atmosphere from about 280 parts per million to about 383 parts per million since 1850. This change appears to be having an adverse effect on the planet due to global climate change, which will be covered in the next chapter.

WEATHER

Air masses are large areas of air that are of uniform temperature and moisture content. Large air masses form when the weather is stable.

Over warm water, an air mass can form in as quickly as two or three days. Over dry land, it can take as long as two or three weeks to form. Air masses generally take one of four forms—warm and dry, cold and dry, warm and moist, or cold and moist—depending on the type of surface over which they form. When weather conditions become unstable due to wind shifts, an air mass begins to move. Moving air masses cause the weather in their path to change.

Air masses are named for regions over which they form. For instance, air masses that form over water are called maritime air masses. Air masses that form over land are called continental air masses. Air masses that form over the Arctic are called Arctic air masses, while air masses that form over the Antarctic are called Antarctic air masses. These polar air masses usually form in the winter, when warming from the Sun is at a minimum. They have very cold air and very little moisture. The temperature and moisture content of an air mass gives the air a certain density. Cool, moist air has a much higher density than warm, dry air.

When air masses move, they interact at their leading edge with other air masses. The place where different air masses interact is called a front. Fronts can be described as one of four types—**cold fronts, warm fronts, occluded fronts, and stationary fronts**. The arrival of a front in an area indicates a change in the weather. For example, as warm air cools, it cannot hold as much moisture, so the excess forms clouds and eventually falls as precipitation—rain, snow, or sleet.

Cold fronts form when the leading edge of a cold air mass moves into a warmer air mass. These fronts typically produce thunderstorms followed by cooler, drier weather. Warm fronts form when the leading edge of a warm air mass overtakes a cooler air mass. Warm fronts typically bring clouds and scattered showers. An occluded front forms when a cold air mass overtakes the leading edge of a warm front. This usually creates scattered rain showers. A stationary front occurs when a moving air mass stalls and stops moving. This usually brings clouds and prolonged precipitation.

Figure 2.3   Cirrus clouds (a) indicate fair weather. Cumulonimbus clouds (b) bring heavy precipitation.

Clouds and Precipitation

Clouds form when **water vapor** in the air condenses into tiny water droplets or ice crystals. The water vapor condenses onto tiny particles called *condensation nuclei.* A condensation nucleus may be a particle of dust, salt, or smoke. While water vapor often changes from a gaseous state to a liquid state as it condenses, sometimes it may change directly to a solid crystalline state. The droplets or ice crystals that make up clouds are very small. They have a radius of about 1×10^{-5} m. Even though these droplets are tiny, when combined they may form clouds with a mass of several million metric tons.

Clouds form in three main ways. First of all, when air is cooled, its ability to hold water vapor decreases. When the point is reached where the air is holding all the water vapor it can hold, the air is said to be saturated. If further cooling takes place, the water vapor condenses from the air to form clouds. This type of cloud formation usually takes place along fronts, in regions where air rises and cools as it goes over mountains, or when warm, moist air moves over a cold surface.

Clouds may also form when two air masses that are below their saturation point mix. This mixing lowers the temperature of the

CONDENSING WATER VAPOR

A quick experiment can be performed to see how much water vapor is in the atmosphere. Fill a glass with ice and water. Dry the sides of the glass and set it on the counter. Water droplets will soon form on the outside of the glass. This happens as warm, moist air in the room comes in contact with the cold surface of the glass. The air that touches the surface of the glass cools below the saturation point of the water vapor and water droplets form on the outside of the glass. On a humid day, the amount of water that condenses is great. On a drier day, when the humidity is very low, only a small amount of water droplets form.

warm air mass to the point where its water vapor condenses. This is the same process that occurs when, on a cold day, you can see your breath in the air.

The third way clouds form is when air absorbs more water vapor at a constant temperature and reaches the saturation point. This happens as an air mass moves over a large body of water such as an ocean or very large lake. In the winter, this occurs as cold Arctic air moves across the warmer waters of the Great Lakes, causing very heavy snowfall next to the lake.

Clouds are dynamic. Water droplets within a cloud are constantly condensing and evaporating. Water droplets also are heavier than air, and as they fall they may evaporate. This cycle of water through the gas-liquid phase changes constantly. These changes, however, occur at the same rate, so the cloud remains in equilibrium. Sometimes, the rate at which water vapor condenses exceeds the rate at which it evaporates. When this happens, water droplets increase in size.

When the water droplets become so large they cannot remain suspended in a cloud, they begin to fall, or precipitate. If the precipitation reaches the ground as a liquid, it is called rain. If the precipitation freezes as it falls, it is called sleet. If the water vapor condenses as ice crystals, and it remains as ice crystals as it falls to the ground, the precipitation is called snow.

ADDRESSING ATMOSPHERIC PROBLEMS

The atmosphere is a dynamic part of Earth's systems. The gases in the atmosphere interact with, and are influenced by, the oceans, the land, and the organisms living on Earth. The atmosphere is also where many important chemical reactions take place. Some of these chemical reactions occur naturally while others are caused by human activity. Humans also have an influence over some of the naturally occurring reactions, because human activity has affected the balances within the system.

Chemical Processes in the Atmosphere

Earth's atmosphere is very dynamic. Its composition has changed over time and is still changing. The amount of water vapor present in the atmosphere is important in both causing weather and removing atmospheric particles. The atmosphere is made up of different gases. Sometimes these different gases react with one another. These reactions may have both positive and negative effects on the Earth.

THE ATMOSPHERE AND LIFE

Earth is well suited to life as we know it. The other planets in our solar system do not have the same characteristics to support life as does Earth. The atmosphere is one of these important characteristics. Oxygen is a vital element for both plants and animals. It is part of the chemical process called respiration by which organisms derive energy from food. A few organisms derive energy from other processes, such as breaking down hydrogen sulfide, but using oxygen is the most prevalent.

Oxygen is not the only important gas in the atmosphere. Plants use carbon dioxide as a building block for food molecules that both plants and animals break down during respiration. Nitrogen in the atmosphere is part of the nitrogen cycle that provides nutrients to plants for making food.

Another vital component to life on Earth is liquid water. Liquid water is part of the hydrosphere. The reason, however, that Earth has abundant liquid water is due to the atmosphere. The atmosphere keeps Earth warm enough that water can remain a liquid.

WARMING THE EARTH

Energy from the Sun warms the Earth. This warming is easily observed by standing in the sunlight on a sunny day—the Sun's energy warms you quickly. On a much broader level, the Sun's energy warms the Earth's surface. Energy is absorbed by the Earth's surface during the day and then radiates outward at night. Some of the gases in the atmosphere trap this radiated energy and prevent it from escaping into space. The atmosphere itself absorbs some solar energy and slowly releases it into space, and it also reflects some solar energy back into space before it reaches the surface.

Earth's Radiation Budget, shown in Figure 3.1, is the balance between incoming energy from the Sun and the outgoing long wave (thermal) and reflected shortwave energy from Earth. This diagram shows the percentages of the incoming solar energy that are reflected, absorbed, and radiated back into space. As you can see in the diagram, the atmosphere plays an important role in all of these processes.

How does the atmosphere, a solution of gases, absorb heat? The main components of the atmosphere are nitrogen and oxygen. These gases are transparent to incoming light energy and outgoing infrared radiation. The heat-absorbing qualities of the atmosphere are caused mainly by some of the trace gases in the atmosphere. These gases

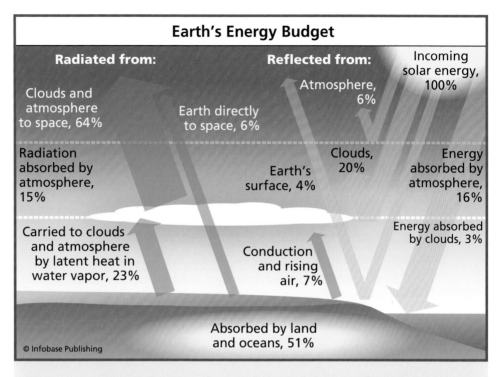

Earth's Energy Budget

Radiated from:

Reflected from:

Incoming solar energy, 100%

Clouds and atmosphere to space, 64%

Earth directly to space, 6%

Atmosphere, 6%

Radiation absorbed by atmosphere, 15%

Earth's surface, 4%

Clouds, 20%

Energy absorbed by atmosphere, 16%

Carried to clouds and atmosphere by latent heat in water vapor, 23%

Conduction and rising air, 7%

Energy absorbed by clouds, 3%

Absorbed by land and oceans, 51%

© Infobase Publishing

Figure 3.1   This diagram shows how energy is absorbed or reflected by the Earth's surface and the atmosphere. The recycling of energy between the Earth's surface and the atmosphere is characteristic of the greenhouse effect. The total energy entering the Earth is equal to the energy leaving Earth, as should be expected for a system in balance.

include water vapor (H_2O), carbon dioxide (CO_2), **chlorofluorocarbons** (**CFCs**), methane (CH_4), nitrous oxide (NO), and ozone (O_3). These gases are commonly called greenhouse gases.

The Greenhouse Effect

The greenhouse effect is Earth's natural heating process. Greenhouse gases allow radiant energy from the Sun to pass through Earth's atmosphere and warm its surface. These same gases prevent heat from escaping into space by absorbing the infrared radiation. This traps heat energy in the atmosphere and warms the planet. If you have ever gotten into a car with all the windows rolled up on a sunny day, you know that the interior of the car is much warmer than the air outside. This is similar to the way the greenhouse effect works. In the car, radiant energy passes through the windows to the car's interior, where it is absorbed and changed to thermal (heat) energy. The windows prevent that thermal energy from escaping. In the atmosphere, the greenhouse gases absorb the heat energy and keep it from escaping. This warms the atmosphere and Earth's surface.

Greenhouse gases make up a tiny portion of gases in the atmosphere. However, they have a big effect on temperature. If Earth's atmosphere were made up of only nitrogen and oxygen, the average temperature at Earth's surface would be about 0°F (–18°C). The temperature would also vary greatly between night and day. Because of the greenhouse gases in the atmosphere, Earth's average temperature is 59°F (15°C). The temperatures do not vary much between night and day compared to the enormous daily temperature fluctuations on planets without atmospheres like Earth's. For example, the surface temperature on the Moon can range from –387°F (–233°C) at night to 253°F (123°C) during the day. The warming due to the greenhouse gases enables Earth to have liquid water and to support life.

As previously mentioned, the concentration of carbon dioxide in the atmosphere has been increasing over the past 150 years. The rise in levels of carbon dioxide and other greenhouse gases is due mainly to human activity. In fact, carbon dioxide is now at the highest level it has been in the past 650,000 years. Scientists have learned this by analyzing the bubbles trapped in Antarctic ice cones over many centuries, providing a window into the atmospheric conditions of the past.

The possibility of global warming due to increasing greenhouse gases was first recognized more than 100 years ago by the Swedish chemist Svante Arrhenius. Arrhenius is famous for his many contributions to modern physical chemistry and acid-base theory. Arrhenius predicted that doubling the concentration of carbon dioxide in the atmosphere would increase Earth's surface temperature by a couple of degrees.

The concentration of atmospheric carbon dioxide has been steadily increasing since about 1850. This time marks the beginning of the Industrial Revolution. One of the side effects of the Industrial Revolution was the burning of coal as an energy source. This led to the use of petroleum and natural gas as energy sources later in the twentieth century. Coal, petroleum, and natural gas are called **fossil fuels**. Fossil fuels contain carbon that was removed from the atmosphere millions of years ago. Sometimes during the carbon cycle, carbon is removed and sequestered, or stored, for very long periods of time. It is currently believed that fossil fuels were formed when ancient organisms died and piled up under extreme heat and pressure, storing up carbon in the process. When these fossil fuels are burned, the stored carbon is released back into the environment

CARBON DIOXIDE AND FOSSIL FUEL COMBUSTION

In a combustion reaction, the products are carbon dioxide and water. As a result, when fossil fuels are burned, carbon dioxide is released. Have you ever wondered how much carbon dioxide is released when gasoline is burned?

- One gallon (3.8 liters) of gasoline weighs 6.3 pounds (2.9 kg). When it is burned, it produces about 20 pounds (9 kg) of carbon dioxide.
- Gasoline is about 87% carbon and 13% hydrogen by weight. Thus, the carbon in a gallon of gasoline weighs 5.5 pounds (6.3 lbs. × .87).

as carbon dioxide. The excess carbon overwhelms the carbon cycle and remains in the atmosphere. This causes the concentration of carbon dioxide to increase in the atmosphere.

Carbon dioxide is the main greenhouse gas of concern because it has a relatively long life in the atmosphere. Scientists believe that carbon dioxide in the atmosphere may remain there, acting as a greenhouse gas, for 50 to 400 years. Methane is actually a more potent greenhouse gas—meaning that it has a greater ability to absorb heat—but it only remains in the atmosphere for about 15 years. As a result, methane has a lower long-term affect on the atmosphere than carbon dioxide. However, all greenhouse gases are considered a problem in the atmosphere.

The Greenhouse Effect and Global Warming

Today, few scientists doubt that increasing carbon dioxide levels cause global warming. The question is how much warming is caused by the increasing greenhouse gases and how much by natural climatic variations. The answer to the question is actually quite complex. Global climate is a result of various **forcings**. Forcings are factors that affect the climate. Forcings may be either positive or negative.

Positive forcings stimulate the warming of Earth's temperature while negative forcings stimulate cooling. These forcings—both positive and negative—are often part of feedback loops. For example, if carbon dioxide levels increase in the atmosphere, Earth becomes warmer (positive forcing). The warming of Earth increases evaporation as part of the hydrologic cycle, adding more water vapor to the atmosphere (positive forcing). However, increased water vapor leads to more cloud cover that reflects heat energy, preventing it from reaching Earth's surface (negative forcing). The clouds also reflect and absorb heat, in the form of infrared radiation, that is escaping from the surface (positive forcing). It is difficult to determine whether the positive forcings are stronger than the negative forcings.

Scientists are not able to experimentally determine the effects of all the forcing because a complete model of Earth cannot be created. Scientists explore the magnitude of positive and negative forcings by using **computer models**. Computer models are simulations that allow scientists to change factors to view the outcomes. Computer models are constantly improving, but they are not perfect. Because of the small amount of uncertainty in computer models and the inability to perform first hand experiments on the exact Earth model, there is some skepticism about global warming.

Ozone

Ozone (O_3) is a molecule made up of three oxygen atoms bonded together. Ozone has a distinctive, pungent smell. Electric motors and electric sparks can produce ozone. Most of the ozone in the stratosphere is confined to a region about 6 to 25 miles (10 to 40 km) above the Earth's surface. This region is called the ozone layer.

The ozone layer is important because ozone molecules absorb ultraviolet radiation coming in from the Sun and prevent ultraviolet radiation from reaching the Earth's surface. Ultraviolet radiation is damaging to plant and animal tissue and is what causes human skin to tan or burn. In fact, overexposure or long-term exposure to ultraviolet radiation can lead to skin cancer in humans. The application of ultraviolet radiation is one method used to kill microorganisms in water during purification.

In the stratosphere, ozone forms when ultraviolet radiation in sunlight causes an oxygen molecule (O_2) to decompose into two oxygen ions (O^-). Each of these ions reacts with an oxygen molecule to form an ozone molecule (O_3). When an ozone molecule absorbs ultraviolet radiation, it decomposes into an oxygen molecule (O_2) and an oxygen ion (O^-). This process continues repeatedly.

Good and Bad Ozone

Ozone located in the ozone layer is considered "good" ozone. The ozone layer absorbs most of the ultraviolet radiation and prevents it from reaching Earth. However, ozone found in the troposphere, the lowest level of the atmosphere, is considered "bad" ozone.

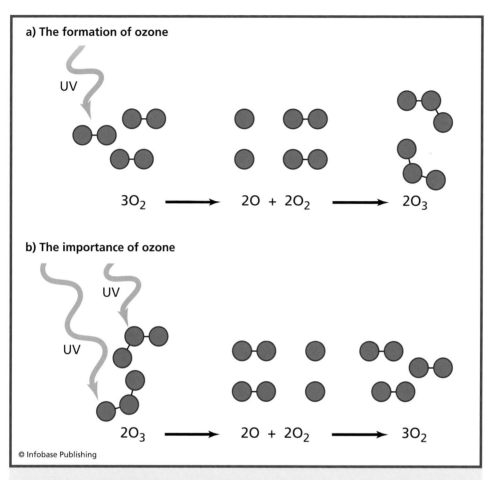

a) The formation of ozone

UV

$3O_2 \longrightarrow 2O + 2O_2 \longrightarrow 2O_3$

b) The importance of ozone

UV

UV

$2O_3 \longrightarrow 2O + 2O_2 \longrightarrow 3O_2$

© Infobase Publishing

Figure 3.2   In the stratosphere there are two forms of oxygen: normal oxygen, O_2, consisting of two O atoms; and ozone, O_3, consisting of three O atoms. UV light is required to transform oxygen into ozone. The O-O bond of an oxygen molecule is broken by the energy from the UV light. Each O atom reacts with oxygen and forms ozone. In a similar way, ozone is destroyed by UV light. In this case the formed O atom reacts with another ozone molecule and forms two oxygen molecules O_2. This process absorbes UV light and prevents it from reaching the Earth' surface.

This "bad" ozone causes problems because it is highly reactive and damages plant and animal tissues. It is sometimes used to sterilize water to kill microorganisms. Ozone is one of the components of smog—air pollution—commonly seen as a haze above large cities. Ozone is also a greenhouse gas.

Ozone is produced in the troposphere when different compounds react with ultraviolet radiation that reaches that level. These compounds include hydrocarbons and nitrogen oxides, which are emitted by automobiles, gasoline vapors, fossil fuel power plants, refineries, and certain other industries. In this way, humans contribute greatly to the production of ozone in the troposphere and it is considered a pollutant.

Ozone Depletion

Compounds containing chlorine, hydrogen, and nitrogen destroy ozone naturally. Chlorine compounds in the atmosphere come from the ocean, hydrogen compounds come from decomposition of water, and nitrogen compounds come from the soil and the oceans. These different natural compounds form in different seasons and cause seasonal changes in ozone concentrations in the troposphere. These compounds seldom affect the ozone in the ozone layer. Natural events, however, such as volcanic eruptions sometimes send these compounds into the stratosphere. The compounds then break down the ozone in the ozone layer, causing an increase in the amount of ultraviolet radiation reaching Earth.

Human activity has also had an affect on the ozone in the stratosphere. A class of compounds called chlorofluorocarbons (CFCs) is used in air conditioning, refrigeration units, and as an aerosol spray propellant. CFCs were discovered in 1920s and were thought to be safe because they were stable and chemically inert. When CFCs rise through the troposphere, however, they are broken down by ultraviolet radiation. The chlorine released from this process destroys ozone. The reaction takes place in three steps as shown in these formulas (where $CFCl_3$ represents chlorofluorocarbons):

$$CFCl_3 + \textit{UV light} \rightarrow CFCl_2 + Cl$$

$$Cl + O_3 \rightarrow ClO + O_2$$

$$ClO + O \rightarrow Cl + O_2$$

The chlorine released in the third step is not broken down or changed, so it continues reacting with ozone as fast as the ozone is produced. Chlorine was not known to affect ozone in the stratosphere until 1973. Scientists found conclusive evidence of

THE OZONE HOLE

In 1984, scientists announced the discovery of an ozone hole over Antarctica. This phenomenon was traced to ozone-depleting chemicals such as CFCs. The ozone hole was touted as a harbinger of what was to become of the ozone layer worldwide. Thanks to efforts to reduce ozone-depleting chemicals, the ozone layer is mending itself. The ozone hole,

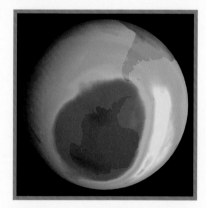

Figure 3.3   The dark inner-blue area shows the hole in the ozone layer.

however, has continued to persist. More than 20 years after its discovery, the ozone hole still covers an area of about 24 million square kilometers—about the size of North America. Scientists are still trying to determine why the ozone hole persists, even though the ozone layer is regenerating.

ozone depletion in 1984. Widespread depletion over the South Pole was discovered in 1985. Soon after, many CFCs were either banned or highly regulated. As a result, ozone levels in the stratosphere have begun to rise again.

Air Pollution

Air pollution is anything that changes the natural characteristics of the atmosphere. Air pollution can change air either chemically or physically. Some types of air pollution, like smoke, are visible. Others, like carbon dioxide, are invisible. Some pollutants are gases that dissolve in air while others are actually particles suspended in air. **Smoke** is made up of solid and/or liquid **particulates**—solid or liquid particles suspended in a gas—and gases resulting from combustion. Depending on the type of combustible materials, the smoke may contain soot (made up of carbon particles), a variety of organic compounds, and even heavy metals.

Smoke may combine with fog to form **smog**, which is often seen as a brownish or yellowish haze over cities. Smog forms as a result of photochemical reactions set in motion when compounds in the smoke react with water droplets in fog in the presence of sunlight. Smog is common in summer in the skies over larger cities. Smog may also cause health problems, such as respiratory distress. Smog can worsen medical conditions such as emphysema, bronchitis, and asthma. Due to the Clean Air Act, which was passed in 1963 with various updates since then, air pollution in the United States has become a manageable problem.

Sulfur Dioxide

Petroleum and coal contain more than just hydrogen and carbon. They also contain trace amounts of sulfur. When coal is burned, the sulfur is converted to sulfur dioxide (SO_2) and released into the atmosphere. Sulfur dioxide is also released during volcanic eruptions or through volcanic vents. In the atmosphere, sulfur dioxide can react with fog to form yellowish **vog**. Vog, like smog, causes respiratory problems.

Sulfur dioxide particles in the atmosphere react with water droplets to create aerosols. The resulting sulfur dioxide aerosols in the atmosphere have a pronounced effect on global climate. They have a negative forcing effect, which means that they cause cooling because these aerosols reflect solar energy back into space before it can warm the atmosphere. Volcanic eruptions often send large amounts of sulfur dioxide into the upper troposphere or into the stratosphere. The cooling effects of a large volcanic eruption may last for several years.

Acid Precipitation

Sulfur dioxide in the lower troposphere also presents another problem. The sulfur dioxide aerosols readily react through a series of chemical reactions with the abundant water droplets in clouds to form acids. These reactions are summarized below:

Sulfur dioxide is oxidized by a reaction with the hydroxyl radical:

$$SO_2 + OH^- \rightarrow HOSO_2^-$$

which is followed by:

$$HOSO_2^- + O_2 \rightarrow HO_2^- + SO_3$$

In the presence of water, sulfur trioxide (SO_3) is converted rapidly to sulfuric acid:

$$SO_3(g) + H_2O(l) \rightarrow H_2SO_4(l)$$

The sulfuric acid produced in the final reaction is dissolved in the water droplets. Under the proper conditions, these droplets come together to form raindrops. These acidified raindrops create a phenomenon called **acid rain** or acid precipitation. This acidic precipitation can damage plants, animals, bodies of water, and manmade structures. Acid precipitation is an ongoing problem in regions that are located downwind from coal-fired electric plants. Acid precipitation has caused numerous streams and ponds in some parts of the United States to become so acidic that they cannot support fish and other aquatic animals and plants. Acid precipitation leeches minerals from the soil and leaves the soil too acidic for use in agriculture.

Sulfur dioxide is not the only compound responsible for acid precipitation. When fossil fuels are burned, the high temperatures produced cause nitrogen in the atmosphere to form nitrogen dioxide (NO_2). In the atmosphere, nitrogen dioxide reacts with water to form nitric acid (HNO_3), as shown in the following reaction:

$$3NO_2 + H_2O \rightarrow 2HNO_3 + NO$$

Beginning in the 1970s, efforts have been made to reduce sulfur dioxide and nitrogen dioxide emissions. Through a combined effort of using only low-sulfur fossil fuels along with technology to remove sulfur dioxide and nitrogen dioxide from smoke before it leaves the plant, emissions of these gases have been greatly reduced.

Protecting the Atmosphere

This chapter has touched on some of the problems facing the atmosphere that are caused by humans. Humans depend on the atmosphere, not only for the air we breathe, but also because it is part of the dynamic Earth systems of biogeochemical cycles. Human activities often create or enhance a number of problems. Many of these have been identified and, once a solution has been found, the problems have been reduced. The atmosphere is dynamic, and various means to clean and maintain it are available. Most of the problems caused by humans result from the overloading of natural cycles or normal conditions. The result is that the atmosphere attains a new equilibrium that is not always favorable to humans.

The Hydrosphere

The hydrosphere consists of all the water that is present above, on, or below Earth's surface. This includes water in solid, liquid, and gaseous states. Solid water, or ice, is found at the polar ice caps, in glaciers, as snow, and as permafrost in soil. Liquid water is found in the ocean, rivers, lakes, underground, and as tiny droplets that make up clouds. Gaseous water occurs in the water vapor in the atmosphere. The total mass of the hydrosphere is about 3.1×10^{21} pounds (1.4×10^{21} kilograms), which is about 0.023% of the Earth's total mass.

Most of the water on Earth is in liquid form. About 70.8% of Earth's surface is covered by water. When viewed from space, the oceans are a striking feature. In fact, Earth is often referred to as "the water planet" or "the blue planet." About 97% of all the Earth's water is found in the oceans as saltwater. Only 3% of the Earth's water is not salty.

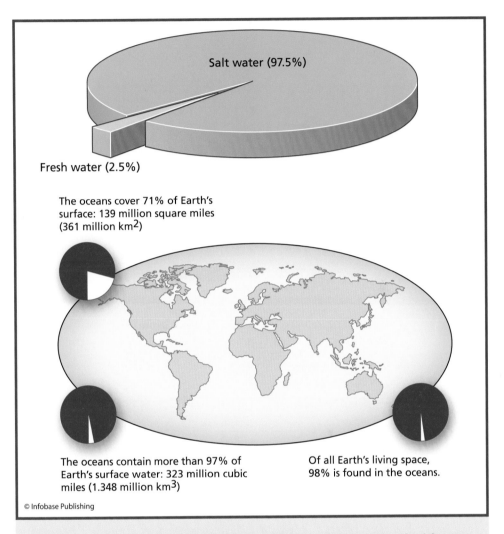

Salt water (97.5%)

Fresh water (2.5%)

The oceans cover 71% of Earth's surface: 139 million square miles (361 million km^2)

The oceans contain more than 97% of Earth's surface water: 323 million cubic miles (1.348 million km^3)

Of all Earth's living space, 98% is found in the oceans.

© Infobase Publishing

Figure 4.1   More than two-thirds of the Earth's surface is covered with water. The vast size and depth of the oceans account for most of the planet's water— therefore, most of the water on Earth is saltwater.

The oceans are made up of water containing dissolved salts. Sodium ions and chloride ions are most abundant in seawater. The average depth of the oceans is 2.4 miles (3.8 km). The maximum depth is found in ocean trenches and reaches about 6.2 miles

Figure 4.2 When viewed from space, the oceans of water are striking in appearance. This gives Earth the nickname "the water planet."

(10 km). The oceans' great depth and broad expanse add up to a volume of over 319 million cubic miles (1,340 million cubic kilometers).

THE ORIGIN AND EVOLUTION OF THE HYDROSPHERE

The hydrosphere covers much of the Earth's surface and contains a very large volume of water. Even though liquid water is one of the unique things about Earth when compared to the other planets in our solar system, scientists are still not entirely sure about where the water came from.

Geologists theorize that liquid water was abundant beginning very early in geologic time. Some of the oldest known rocks are sedimentary rocks more than 4 billion years old. Because erosion and deposition are involved with the formation of sedimentary rocks, it is likely that water was present when these very old rocks formed. Some geologists theorize that early in geologic time, volcanic eruptions ejected large amounts of water vapor into the atmosphere. Much of the water vapor condensed and turned to liquid water, forming early oceans on Earth. Other scientists suggests that most water on Earth came from extraterrestrial sources such as comets. They theorize that massive amounts of water were brought by the comets that bombarded Earth early in the planet's history.

Regardless of the source of the water, the oceans have been a prominent feature on Earth for most of its history. As already mentioned, the ocean water is salty. These salts come from the lithosphere. Because water is a great solvent, it has the ability to dissolve the salts from rocks and soil and transport them to the oceans. This process has been transporting salts to the ocean for all of geologic time.

The oceans do not become more salty over time, because there are processes that remove the salts from solution. Calcium ions are removed from seawater mainly by living organisms that use the calcium to make shells. Organisms that make shells range from microscopic organisms to shellfish such as clams and oysters and corals. These organisms remove calcium from the water and absorb it into their shells. When these organisms die, they settle to the ocean floor. Over time, their shells are covered with sediments and become part of the lithosphere. Salts made of sodium ions are removed from seawater as they are adsorbed by clay particles suspended in the ocean waters. As these clay particles fall to the ocean floor, they too are buried and become part of the lithosphere.

PHYSICAL AND CHEMICAL PROPERTIES OF WATER

Water is a very common chemical compound on Earth. This compound consists of two hydrogen atoms bonded with an oxygen atom. The chemical formula for water is H_2O. Water may also be called dihydrogen oxide or hydrogen, but these names are rarely used. The term *water* specifically refers to the compound in the liquid state. The solid state is called ice and the gaseous state is called water vapor. On Earth, all three phases are common, with the liquid form being the most common.

The two hydrogen atoms bonded to the oxygen molecule give water one of its special chemical properties: polarity. Because of the shape of the molecule, the hydrogen atoms give one "end" of the molecule a partial positive charge. Two unshared pairs of electrons

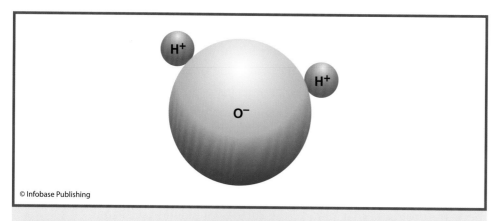

© Infobase Publishing

Figure 4.3   Water has a simple molecular structure. It is composed of one oxygen atom and two hydrogen atoms. Each hydrogen atom is covalently bonded to the oxygen via a shared pair of electrons. Oxygen also has two unshared pairs of electrons. Water is a "polar" molecule because there is an uneven distribution of electron density. Water has a partial negative charge near the oxygen atom due to the unshared pairs of electrons, and partial positive charges near the hydrogen atoms.

on the oxygen atom give the other "end" of the molecule a partial negative charge. This arrangement makes water a polar molecule, so it can attract both positive and negative charges. Because water molecules are polar, they attract each other. This gives water several unique properties.

The **cohesive forces** between molecules in a liquid are shared with all neighboring atoms. Those molecules at the surface of a liquid have no neighboring atoms above them. This arrangement results in stronger attractive forces on the other molecules at the surface. The increased intermolecular attractive forces at the surface produce **surface tension**.

When attractive forces are exerted between unlike molecules, they are said to be **adhesive forces**. As an example, consider water in a glass tube. The adhesive forces between water molecules and the walls of the glass tube are stronger than the cohesive forces between adjacent molecules of water. This greater attraction leads to an upward turning *meniscus* (curved upper surface) of the water surface at the walls of the vessel and contributes to **capillary action**. Capillary action makes it possible for water and nutrients to rise up from the underground roots of plants to nourish the rest of the plants.

Water and Heat

A relatively small mass of water can absorb large amounts of heat. This property is called **specific heat capacity**. Liquid water absorbs 4.18 joules per gram of heat (a joule is a unit of energy) to raise its temperature by 1.8°F (1°C). Compared to many substances, such as iron, which has a specific heat capacity of 0.450 J/g, water has a high specific heat capacity. In fact, water has the second highest heat capacity of all known substances. This means that water must absorb a large amount of energy before its temperature rises, and it must lose a large amount of energy before its temperature decreases. This property of water is beneficial to helping maintain Earth's temperature. This is why being near a large body of water helps to moderate temperatures. The water absorbs heat during the day and prevents the temperature of the surrounding air from rising too fast. At night, heat is slowly released from the water, warming the surrounding air and preventing the temperature from falling too low.

States of Water

Under standard conditions of temperature and pressure (STP), water has a **melting point** of 32°F (0°C) and a **boiling point** of 212°F (100°C). At 68°F (20°C), the **density** of water is 0.998 g/cm^3 and the density of ice is 0.92 g/cm^3. Water reaches it maximum density at 39°F (4°C). At that temperature, the density of water is 1.000 g/cm^3. Because ice is less dense than water, it floats in water. This is a unique property of water because the density of most elements and compounds is greatest when they are in their solid state.

Water molecules are attracted to each other by weak chemical bonds between the positively charged hydrogen atoms and the negatively charged oxygen atoms of neighboring water molecules. These bonds are called hydrogen bonds. As water cools below 39°F (4°C), the hydrogen bonds adjust to "push" the negatively charged oxygen atoms apart. This action produces a crystal lattice we know as ice.

Ice floats because it is about 9% less dense than liquid water. In other words, ice takes up about 9% more space than water, so a liter of ice weighs less than a liter of water. The denser water displaces the less dense ice, so ice floats on top of water. As a result, lakes and rivers freeze from top to bottom, allowing fish to survive even when the surface of a lake has frozen over. If ice were denser than water, it would sink. The liquid water would be displaced to the top and exposed to the colder temperature. If such were the case, all bodies of water would freeze from the bottom up.

Water has the ability to dissolve many different substances. Water causes many salts to **dissociate** into ions. When salts dissociate, they break up into positive and negative ions. For example, sodium chloride (NaCl), which is common table salt, dissociates in water to form positive sodium ions (Na^+) and negative chloride ions (Cl^-). Water also dissolves many non-ionic compounds. One example is sucrose ($C_{12}H_{22}O_{11}$), which is common table sugar. When added to water, the sucrose does not break into ions like the table salt. Instead, the bonds that hold sucrose molecules together break apart, producing individual molecules that disperse throughout the water.

Because it can dissolve so many different substances, water is sometimes called the universal **solvent**. The ability of water to dissolve so many different substances makes it an important agent in chemical weathering. As water dissolves substances, it can take on differing chemical properties—for instance, it can become an acid or a base. This further enhances water as a chemical weathering agent.

Properties of Freshwater

Fresh water makes up only about 3% of all the water on Earth. Fresh water includes surface water, groundwater, and all ice. The most familiar fresh water is found in lakes and under the ground. These sources are commonly used for drinking water. Lakes, rivers, and groundwater are a part of the hydrologic cycle. As water vapor condenses in the atmosphere and falls as precipitation, the droplets remove dust from the air. In this way, water cleans particulates from the atmosphere.

When the precipitation falls on Earth's land surface, some of it runs off across the surface to form streams. Streams converge to form rivers. Sometimes, rivers are impounded, or enclosed, and widen into lakes. Lakes form both naturally or when dams are constructed.

Some water seeps into the ground through cracks, fractures, fissures, and caves to become groundwater. Groundwater is important for the storage of fresh water. In many parts of the world, groundwater is an important source of drinking water. Groundwater returns to the surface through water wells or through springs. As water flows over or under the ground, it dissolves chemical compounds from minerals. These chemical compounds have different effects on the water before it reaches the ocean.

Water dissolves minerals from the rocks. Different types of minerals have different chemical compositions. As a result, water at different locations is exposed to different types of minerals. This affects the minerals that are dissolved in the water. These differences account for different properties and even taste. Water is sometimes referred to as "hard" or "soft." Hard water has a high dissolved mineral content, while soft water does not. The most familiar difference between hard water and soft water is how well it allows soap to lather. In hard water, soap does not lather well. In soft water, soap lathers well and is hard to rinse away.

The amount of minerals dissolved in water determines the water's **hardness**. The hardness of water is due mainly to the presence of calcium and magnesium ions in the water. Calcium and magnesium are common in many different minerals. In some areas, because of the geology of the rocks, manganese, iron, or aluminum may be the main metal ions that cause hardness. Scientists report the total hardness of water in milligrams per liter (mg/L) of calcium carbonate ($CaCO_3$).

Hard water can cause problems due to its high mineral content. Water heaters, cooling towers, and industrial boilers have problems with the minerals precipitating out of the water and forming scale. Scale is a hard mineral coating that can completely clog pipes after some time. The inside of a well-used teakettle has whitish deposits of scale that have been deposited as water was boiled. The relative hardness of water is determined by these guidelines:

- Soft: 0–20 mg/L as calcium
- Moderately soft: 20–40 mg/L as calcium
- Slightly hard: 40–60 mg/L as calcium
- Moderately hard: 60–80 mg/L as calcium
- Hard: 80–120 mg/L as calcium
- Very hard: >120 mg/L as calcium

The type and amount of minerals dissolved in water depend on several factors. In general, warm water is more effective at dissolving minerals than cold water. Waters heated deep underground by volcanic rocks and gases may contain a wide variety of dissolved minerals. As the water cools, the minerals are no longer able to be held in solution, and they precipitate out of the water to produce unusual forms and unusual minerals.

Acid or Base

Another factor that affects the type and quantity of minerals dissolved in water is whether the water is **acidic** or **basic**. Acidic water has compounds dissolved in it that give it the properties of an acid. Basic water, or alkaline water, contains dissolved compounds that give it the properties of a base. The measure of the acidity or alkalinity of water is called **pH**. Most substances have a pH that ranges from 1 to 14. A pH of 7 is considered neutral—neither acidic nor basic. Solutions with a pH of less than 7 are considered acidic, while those with a pH greater than 7 are considered basic.

The pH of water is an important factor in the minerals it dissolves. Some minerals will only dissolve in acidic waters while others will only dissolve in basic waters. Acidic waters are typically better at dissolving **heavy metals**, such as mercury (Hg), cadmium (Cd), arsenic (As), chromium (Cr), thallium (Tl), and lead (Pb). These metals can be harmful to living organisms because they tend to build up in the body and interfere with critical biological functions. Each heavy metal affects different **biological pathways**. Heavy metals affect both plants and animals. Not all heavy metals are bad. Many biological pathways depend on specific heavy metals. Human blood is dependent on iron in the hemoglobin to carry oxygen throughout the body. Too much iron can also cause problems, however.

Acid precipitation, or acid rain, is a problem because acidic water is able to dissolve heavy metals. These heavy metals can pose problems with organisms, such as fish and plants living in rivers and lakes. The heavy metals may also pose a problem to humans when the water is used for drinking. Removing heavy metals from drinking water is often difficult and requires expensive treatment before the water is safe to use.

Properties of Ocean Water

Ocean water is salty. The salts in ocean water are dissolved from rocks and minerals and carried into the sea by rivers. Other minerals are dissolved directly into seawater through erosion and volcanic eruptions. Dust blown by winds or carried by precipitation can also deposit minerals directly to the oceans. The salts in seawater are usually dissociated ions.

The amount of dissolved inorganic salts in water is called **salinity**. Seawater averages about 1.2 ounces (34.4 grams) of salts for each kilogram of water. Salinity is often expressed as a percentage of salt to water. Seawater varies in salinity by its location. Typically, seawater varies from 3.1% to 3.8% salinity. The average salinity of seawater is 3.44%. Salinity will be lower close to the mouth of a river due to the freshwater from the river. In areas such as the Red Sea, where evaporation is high and little freshwater is added by rivers, the salinity is higher. Some isolated lakes can become **hypersaline**. The Dead Sea is a hypersaline lake where salinity approaches 30%. The Great Salt Lake in Utah is another hypersaline lake. The salinity in the Great Salt Lake ranges from 5% to 27%, depending on the lake level.

The concentration of dissolved ions is usually expressed in grams per kilograms (g/kg). Some typical values are: chloride (Cl^-), 19.35 g/kg; sodium (Na^+), 10.78 g/kg; sulfate (SO_4^{2-}), 2.71 g/kg; magnesium (Mg^{2+}), 1.28 g/kg; calcium (Ca^{2+}), 0.71 g/kg; potassium (K^+), 0.40 g/kg; bicarbonate (HCO_3^-), 0.13 g/kg; bromide (Br^-), 0.07 g/kg; and strontium (Sr^{2+}), 0.01 g/kg. Sodium and chloride are the two most common ions found in seawater. The dissolved salts in the water also give seawater a higher density than that of fresh water. While pure water has a density around 1.000 g/cm^3, seawater has a average density of 1.034 g/cm^3.

Sodium chloride is common table salt. It is also found in the blood and other fluids of most multicellular organisms, which makes it an important compound. Most animals get salt through their diets. Humans also use salt for many industrial processes. Salt has traditionally been used for drying foods for long-term storage. Throughout history, people also have depended on sources other than their food for salt. In some areas, ancient oceans evaporated and left behind salt deposits. These were, and still are, mined for their salt.

Another source of salt is the evaporation of seawater, or **brine**. Brine is water saturated, or nearly saturated, with salt. Brine occurs naturally in hypersaline lakes and in some groundwater. To obtain salt from this source, the liquid portion of seawater or brine is allowed to evaporate. As the water evaporates, crystals of salts begin to form. Once the water has evaporated, only crystals of sea salt remain. Seawater and brine are mixtures of many different elements and compounds dissolved in water. All these substances are present

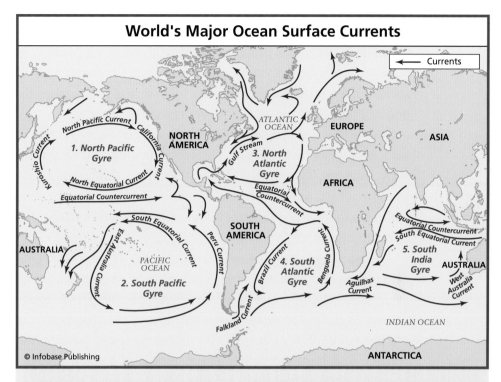

World's Major Ocean Surface Currents

Currents

North Pacific Current
California Current
Kuroshio Current
1. North Pacific Gyre
North Equatorial Current
Equatorial Countercurrent
ATLANTIC OCEAN
NORTH AMERICA
EUROPE
ASIA
Gulf Stream
3. North Atlantic Gyre
AFRICA
Equatorial Countercurrent
South Equatorial Current
East Australia Current
AUSTRALIA
PACIFIC OCEAN
2. South Pacific Gyre
SOUTH AMERICA
Peru Current
Brazil Current
4. South Atlantic Gyre
Benguela Current
Aguilhas Current
Equatorial Countercurrent
South Equatorial Current
5. South India Gyre
AUSTRALIA
West Australia Current
Falkland Current
INDIAN OCEAN
ANTARCTICA
© Infobase Publishing

Figure 4.4   Surface water movement in the oceans takes place in the form of currents. Currents move ocean water horizontally at the ocean's surface. Surface currents are driven mainly by the wind and other forces such as the Coriolis effect. The location of land masses affect surface current patterns, creating huge circular patterns called current gyres. From the equator to middle latitudes, the circular motion is clockwise in the Northern Hemisphere and counterclockwise in the Southern Hemisphere.

in the sea salt crystals. Once recovered, sea salt may be used as is or further refined to remove specific elements or compounds.

The salts dissolved in seawater also affect the freezing point of the water. Pure water freezes at 32°F (0°C), but seawater freezes at a lower temperature. Average seawater freezes at about 28°F (–2°C). Hypersaline water would freeze at 25°F (–4°C) or lower, depending on the salinity. The change in freezing point due to the salt dissolved in the water is a **colligative property**. Colligative properties refer to the changes in physical properties of a liquid due to the presence of dissolved nonvolatile solutes. In seawater, the salts are nonvolatile solutes. The salt in the water lowers the freezing point, raises the boiling point, and changes the vapor pressure of the water.

When seawater freezes, it forms sea ice. The water content of sea ice is largely fresh, because the salt-containing water is pushed away from the water molecules as they form the crystal lattice structure of ice. Sea ice forms at the surface of the water. Ice crystals begin to form and then they come together to form larger and larger chunks of ice.

Ocean waters are constantly on the move. These movements, called currents, influence the global climate. In general, ocean currents move cold waters from the Arctic and Antarctic toward warmer regions and move warm water from the tropics toward the poles. The flow of currents is affected by wind, salinity, heat content, and Earth's rotation. The direction of motion of water currents is affected by Earth's rotation. This is called the Coriolis effect. In the Northern Hemisphere, currents generally flow in a clockwise direction, and in the Southern Hemisphere they flow counterclockwise.

PROCESSES IN THE HYDROSPHERE

Like the atmosphere, the hydrosphere is dynamic. The hydrosphere encompasses the water cycle and is a part of weather and climate. Plants and animals need the hydrosphere for life functions. The hydrosphere helps regulate the temperature of Earth by storing vast amounts of heat energy and slowly releasing it. The actions of humans and of some natural processes do affect the hydrosphere. The next chapter explores some of the problems caused by their actions.

Chemical and Physical Processes in the Hydrosphere

Many chemical processes take place within the hydrosphere. The chemical and physical properties of water allow for many different types of processes that affect Earth. Water also is a powerful agent in weathering and erosion. While these processes take place largely in the hydrosphere, they will be discussed in more detail in the chapters about the lithosphere.

GROUNDWATER

Groundwater is an important resource because it supplies drinking water to many people. To access groundwater, wells are drilled into rock soil to intersect layers where it is found. The water in these layers may be in spaces between particles in the rock, or it may be in cracks, fissures, faults, or caves. Rock units holding groundwater are called **aquifers**.

Recall that water is called the universal solvent, because it can dissolve so many different substances. Many of the rocks where water is found are made of minerals that contain calcium carbonate. One of these types of rocks is limestone. Limestone is made of calcium carbonate that precipitated out of warm tropical oceans in the past and calcium carbonate that makes up shells of organisms. Over time, these sediments solidify into rock.

Water, especially acidic water, can get into the smallest of cracks and slowly enlarge them by dissolving the calcium carbonate in the rocks. As the tiny cracks enlarge, they become connected to other cracks. Over time, these networks of cracks form conduits through which water may pass. As new water is introduced, it dissolves more calcium carbonate.

Limestone is not the only rock that water moves through. Some sandstone deposits also contain bodies of groundwater. Sandstone is made up of sand grains cemented together, usually by calcium carbonate. Because water can dissolve the calcium carbonate, it opens up spaces between the sand grains, allowing water to pass.

Groundwater is similar to the water in rivers and lakes found on the surface. Sometimes, groundwater flows; at other times, it pools, much like a lake. Groundwater may remain underground for a very short time or for many, many years. In some places, groundwater reaches the surface at springs. Groundwater may also be pumped out of the ground at wells. The storage of groundwater underground reduces evaporation, as it is not exposed to sunlight. Groundwater is a vital part of the hydrologic cycle.

The pumping of groundwater out of the ground may cause problems. If the rate at which the water is pumped out exceeds the rate at which it infiltrates the ground, the aquifer will eventually be pumped dry. In some areas, such as parts of Florida, removal of groundwater weakens the rocks and causes them to collapse, producing sinkholes. Near the coast, excessive groundwater pumping allows seawater to move into the aquifer, making the water salty. Excessive development in an area may prevent water from entering an aquifer, leading to a shortage of fresh water. If there is any pollution in the water that enters an aquifer, it may pollute the entire aquifer. Once polluted, groundwater is difficult to clean because it is difficult to reach. These are just a few of the problems associated with groundwater. While groundwater is an excellent water source, it must be protected.

GLACIERS

A glacier is a huge mass of moving ice. Some glaciers, like those in Greenland and Antarctica, are giant sheets of ice, hundreds of feet thick. Most glaciers are slow-moving rivers of ice. Glaciers are formed from compacted layers of snow. While ice is normally brittle, the huge volume of ice in a glacier has a different quality. Ice less than about 165 ft (50 m) in thickness is brittle. Thicker ice exerts enough pressure along its base to create **plastic flow**. Plastic flow is a condition where the ice takes on more of a consistency of clay. The ice slowly oozes downhill, dragging the more brittle ice above along with it. **Basal sliding**, which also facilitates glacial movement, is the sliding of a glacier over a surface lubricated by meltwater. The meltwater reduces friction, making it easier for the glacier to move across the rocky surface below.

The speed at which glaciers move varies. Some glaciers advance, some retreat, and some remain in about the same location. The ice in a glacier is constantly moving downhill. The apparent advance or retreat of the leading edge of a glacier has to do with whether the rate of melting is faster or slower than the rate of advance. The rate of flow of a glacier can reach as high as several feet per day. Most glaciers do not reach such speeds, but there are a number of them that do.

Like rivers, glaciers are agents of erosion. The bottom of a glacier is studded with rocks that it picks up as it moves. These rocks, embedded in the ice, act like sandpaper and scour the terrain that they cross. Glaciers are capable of shaping landscapes into new forms. Glaciers also create gravel deposits called till. As glaciers

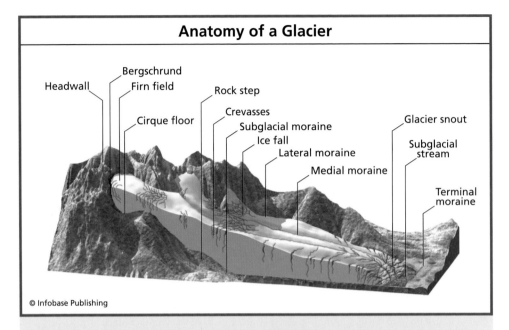

Anatomy of a Glacier

Headwall

Bergschrund

Firn field

Rock step

Cirque floor

Crevasses

Subglacial moraine

Ice fall

Lateral moraine

Medial moraine

Glacier snout

Subglacial stream

Terminal moraine

© Infobase Publishing

Figure 5.1   Glaciers are a dynamic system of moving ice. Glaciers erode materials from one place, carry the eroded material, and deposit it downslope.

grind rock surfaces, they create a fine powder called **rock flour**. After it dries, rock flour can be picked up by wind and carried for long distances. Where the rock flour is deposited, it eventually can form layers as much as several hundred feet thick. Some soils in the midwestern United States and parts of China are made up of these deposits. They are usually very fertile soils and are used widely for agriculture.

Glaciers are made up of large bodies of ice and therefore have a large mass. The mass of some glaciers is so great that it actually depresses the Earth's crust beneath the ice. As these glaciers melt, the pressure from the ice is released and the crust slowly returns to its original position. This slow process is called **isostatic rebound**. For example, the northern part of the North American continent is still rebounding from the weight of the huge ice sheets that covered the area during the last ice age, which ended about 10,000 years ago.

Global warming has caused changes in the world's glaciers. As temperatures change, so do precipitation patterns. Many of the world's glaciers are melting at increasing rates. Due to the rapid melting, isostatic rebound can occur much more quickly. This causes the freshly uncovered rocks to fracture and form small faults. The effects of glaciers on Earth's landscapes will be covered in the next chapter.

EL NIÑO AND LA NIÑA

El Niño and La Niña are two global weather phenomena. They are part of a combined atmospheric-oceanic pattern of climate fluctuation. El Niño and La Niña affect both the oceanic and atmospheric circulation and result in changes to global weather patterns. El Niño is characterized by warmer than normal surface temperatures in the central Pacific Ocean. La Niña is characterized by cooler than normal surface temperatures that also occur in the central Pacific Ocean. Of the two, El Niño has the stronger effect. To be classified as an El Niño, several changes must occur: There must be a rise in air pressure over the Indian Ocean, there must be a drop in air pressure over Tahiti and the eastern Pacific Ocean, and the trade winds must weaken or reverse direction. The combined effect of these changes is that the rising warm air in Peru causes rain in the desert, causing warm water to spread from west to east across the eastern Pacific Ocean.

As warm water moves to the eastern Pacific, it keeps the cold, nutrient-rich waters from rising off the coast of South America. This causes a decline in the fish population, as the lack of nutrients slows the growth of **plankton**. Fishing is an important economic activity in the eastern Pacific. Usually, an El Niño only lasts for a few weeks to a couple of months. When the effects of El Niño decrease, the easterly trade winds return and push away waters from the South

American coast. This allows nutrient-rich deep water to rise. The nutrients provide for plankton growth that attracts fish. When an El Niño event lasts for a longer period of time, it takes longer for the fishing to improve.

An El Niño event has effects beyond the Pacific Ocean basin. For example, South America experiences warmer and wetter summers. North America experiences winters that are warmer than normal in the upper midwest states, the Northeast, and Canada, while California, northwest Mexico, and the southwestern United States are wetter and cooler than normal. Summer is wetter in the intermountain regions of the United States. The Pacific Northwest states tend to experience dry but foggy winters and warm, sunny springs during an El Niño. El Niño also decreases hurricane activity in the Atlantic Ocean. East Africa experiences wetter than normal conditions, and Central Africa has drier than normal conditions.

La Niña also affects the global climate. The cooler than normal waters in the western Pacific Ocean usually has the opposite effect on the global climate as El Niño. The effects of La Niña are not as strong, however.

El Niño and La Niña result from interaction between the surface of the ocean and the atmosphere in the tropical Pacific. Changes in the ocean impact the atmosphere and climate patterns around the globe. In turn, changes in the atmosphere impact ocean temperatures and currents. On average, the system oscillates between warm (El Niño) to neutral (or cold La Niña) conditions every three to four years.

WATER POLLUTION

Water pollution is the contamination of water resources by harmful waste materials produced as a result of human activity. Pollutants are produced by a wide variety of activities. Each pollutant has it own effects, and specific methods must be used to clean up or remove the pollutant. Pollutants include chemicals that make water toxic, chemicals that change the physical characteristics of water, and biological agents.

Toxic chemicals include a vast array that are used for a wide variety of purposes. These substances include pesticides, industrial wastes, fertilizers, petroleum products, and organic solvents. These **contaminants** enter the hydrosphere in many ways. Rainwater runoff washes some materials from land into rivers, lakes, and groundwater. Illegal dumping or improper storage of certain materials also leads to contamination. Even properly stored wastes may eventually leak contaminants into water. Landfills where wastes are stored sometimes leak toxic chemicals into surface water or groundwater.

Pesticides and fertilizers used at home and in agriculture can be washed into surface water or groundwater by rainfall. Petroleum products, such as oil, gas, and diesel, leak from cars and trucks onto roads and driveways. Rain then washes these products into surface-water and groundwater. It is impossible to prevent all contaminants from reaching Earth's waters. There will always be accidents, and some uses of certain materials lead to unavoidable runoff into water supplies. Illegal dumping, improper disposal, and improper use of toxic chemicals are the leading causes of this type of pollution. By proper disposal and use, the risk of these toxic chemicals entering the environment is greatly reduced.

Chemicals that change the physical characteristics of water are also a type of water pollution. Sulfur dioxide and nitrogen dioxide from combustion products lead to acid precipitation. Acid precipitation is rain or snow that has a lower than normal pH. The acid precipitation affects rivers and lakes by lowering their pH and can leach heavy metals from the soil. Another source of acid in the environment comes from mining. Strong acids are formed when some metal minerals break down. These acids commonly seep from mining operations and are carried into rivers and lakes. These acids have the same effect on water as acid precipitation.

Figure 5.2 Pollution degrades water quality by changing the physical characteristics of water. Some pollution is easy to see, as in this photograph. Sometimes chemicals dissolved in the water are invisible but they still have a strong effect on water quality.

Organic debris such as brush, leaves, food processing wastes, and animal feces can also change the physical characteristics of water. These types of wastes can change the taste and smell of water, change the pH, add chemicals, and even add disease-causing organisms, which are also called **pathogens**.

Pathogens released into water by humans and other animals pose a high risk of pollution. Pathogens are often difficult to detect because they are colorless, odorless, and tasteless. To detect pathogens in water, the water must be tested and the pathogens grown in a laboratory. Different pathogens require different conditions, such as temperature and nutrients, to reproduce and to grow. This also takes time, usually 24 hours or more. Because of these factors, scientists look for only a limited number of common microbes that indicate that pathogens might be present. One of the most common microbes tested for is *Escherichia coli*, commonly called *E. coli* or fecal coliform bacteria. Theses bacteria are found in the digestive tracts of all warm-blooded animals and are released in their feces. These feces may also carry pathogens. The test for *E. coli* is easy, so it is used as an indicator of possible pathogen contamination.

Most water pollutants are carried to the oceans by rivers. When some of these pollutants reach the ocean, they become so diluted they no longer present a problem. However, for most other pollutants, the problems they create continue. Many contaminants are absorbed or accumulate in soil and clay particles. Some contaminants decompose to form simpler compounds which may be more toxic than the original material. Finally, some contaminants become part of the food chain and accumulate in the tissues of living organisms.

Chemical Reactions of Pollutants

Most pollutants will take part in chemical reactions. Some pollutants will break down, or decay, when they enter the environment. Sometimes they decay into less toxic, or even nontoxic, chemicals. In other cases, the products of decay are even more toxic than the original material. Chemical decay processes are called **degradable** or **oxi-degradable** processes. Degradable processes depend on sunlight, chemical action, or some other means to speed up or cause decay. Oxi-degradable processes depend on oxygen from the atmosphere to cause a reaction.

Some pollutants are **biodegradable**. Biological processes break down biodegradable materials. The actions of microbes use parts of these substances as food and the result is that the pollutants are broken down into smaller units. Some biodegradable processes take place rapidly, while others are very slow. One such biodegradable material is a special plastic. This plastic has starch from plants incorporated into petroleum-based organic **polymers**. Microbes use the starch as food, thereby breaking the long-chain polymers into shorter chains.

Another common pollutant is fertilizer. Fertilizer is used on agricultural fields to improve crop yield. It also is used for homes and businesses, to improve their yards and landscaping. Rainwater washes fertilizers from these fields and yards into rivers and other bodies of water. When fertilizer enters a river, it adds nutrients to the water, which encourages the growth of aquatic plants. One of the most common types of plant found in rivers and lakes is algae. Fertilizer stimulates rapid and excessive growth in algae and other aquatic plants. The plants take in carbon dioxide to make food. Excessive plant growth uses up the carbon dioxide in the water faster than it can be replaced. This imbalance causes plants to die, and the decay of these plants uses up the dissolved oxygen in the water. Without oxygen, water becomes **anoxic**, and fish and other animals living in it die.

Fertilizers are not the only pollutants that remove oxygen from the water. Some pollutants react with oxygen to leave the waters in some rivers, lakes, and even the ocean, anoxic. Sewage and animal waste also quickly rob water of oxygen. The resulting anoxic conditions cause massive amounts of fish to die. These wastes also contain nutrients used by plants, which further compounds the problem.

Some pollutants, such as certain metals, petroleum, and pesticides, are absorbed by, or accumulate in, clay and soil particles, thereby creating contaminated soils. The contaminated soil can also be eroded and deposited in water resources, thus becoming a water pollution problem, too.

Oil and Petroleum

Oil and other petroleum products are less dense than water, so they float on its surface. A rainbow-colored sheen on the surface of standing water near a street actually consists of oil or other hydrocarbons. Oil is a major cause of pollution because it is so widely used throughout the world. Just one quart of motor oil is enough to pollute 250,000 gallons of water. Oil is spilled, leaked, or otherwise improperly disposed of quite often. The oil is washed from land by rain and into rivers, lakes, groundwater, and the ocean.

Oil eventually will break down, but this takes many years. Oil that is buried in sediments may take a very long time to degrade. Some of the worst oil spills occur when tanker ships that are transporting oil have an accident. The oil quickly spreads over the ocean surface and, if near shore, coats the shoreline. This results in large kills of fish, shorebirds, and marine mammals. These spills also kill many of the other organisms in the area by coating them with oil and toxins. When one of these accidents occurs, it is a major problem to clean up the spill site and restore the habitat. Oil spills are cleaned up by using materials to absorb the oil, by

THE WRECK OF THE EXXON VALDEZ

The oil tanker *Exxon Valdez* ran aground on March 24, 1989. The ship spilled an estimated 11 million gallons of crude oil into Prince William Sound in Alaska. While this was not the largest oil spill in history, it made headlines around the world. The oil spill impacted fish, birds, and marine mammals for many years. Cleanup efforts removed most of the oil from the water and beaches. Today, while the area looks natural again, there are still pockets of oil just beneath the surface on the beaches.

Figure 5.3   A smaller ship attempts to off-load oil from the Exxon Valdez.

skimming the oil off the water's surface, or by using bacteria to biodegrade the oil.

Cleaning Up Water Pollution

The act of cleaning up pollution is called **remediation**. Remediation of water has special requirements to make it effective. The first problems are identifying the source of the pollution and stopping the pollutant from spreading further. Once the source is identified, additional pollutants must be prevented from entering the water. Next, it is important to stop the pollutant from spreading. This presents a challenge to remediation because many pollutants spread quickly in water. Rivers can wash pollutants downstream to the ocean quite rapidly. In many cases, this movement of material downstream is actually one of the most helpful options for treatment. Once the pollutants reach a lake or the ocean, it is possible the large volume of water will dilute the pollutant so that it is no longer a problem.

Water can be removed from a lake or river and treated. This method works for some chemicals but it is difficult for larger bodies or volumes of water. In some cases, additional chemicals may be added to chemically react with the pollutant. Oxidants such as ozone gas, hydrogen peroxide, or potassium permanganate are commonly used. These types of treatments are usually best suited for ponds or small lakes. Adding a basic substance such as lime to neutralize acid may treat the effects of acid drainage.

In some cases, decontaminated water is simply removed for treatment elsewhere. This method only works on small ponds. Pumping water through filters or activated charcoal removes many contaminants. Often, to completely remediate a site, some surrounding sediments need to be removed, as they are also contaminated. Whatever method is chosen to treat surface water, it comes at a considerable cost and it is often difficult to protect the plants and animals that live there.

Groundwater presents many more complicated issues for remediation. When remediating groundwater, the water can be accessed only through wells. The sediments underground cannot be reached, which presents a major challenge for this process.

One method is to pump water out of a well and treat the water with filtration. The type of filtering that is used depends on what contaminants the water contains. This type of treatment works best for groundwater that has been contaminated with hydrocarbons. Depending on the geology of the area's water system, the treatment can quickly reduce high levels of hydrocarbons. The filtered water may be removed or injected back into a well some distance away from where it was pumped.

The use of oxidants also works with groundwater. Because groundwater often flows slowly, oxidants are injected into one well and a large volume of water is pumped out of another nearby well. The pumping well draws the oxidant from the injection well toward the pumping well.

These remediation methods for groundwater only work in very limited areas. If the contamination affects a very large area, the remediation process must be repeated in different locations. Often it is impossible to completely remediate groundwater because contaminants become trapped in the sediments and continue to leach out over time. For these reasons, it is important to protect groundwater to prevent contamination.

Addressing Problems in the Hydrosphere

It is always more difficult to remediate water pollution than it is to prevent it from happening. Even the oceans, with their vast quantities of water, are susceptible to pollution. Preventing water pollution is especially difficult because of how water falls as precipitation all over the planet. This water is exposed to pollutants in both the atmosphere and at Earth's surface. Clean water is a vital resource needed by all living things. For these reasons, protecting the hydrosphere is vital.

The Lithosphere

The *lithosphere* is the rocky, solid outermost shell of Earth. It includes the crust and the upper mantle and is broken up into several tectonic plates that slowly move across the surface of the Earth. These plates ride on the lower portion of the mantle, which is called the *asthenosphere.*

The concept of a lithosphere and an asthenosphere was first established in 1914, when a geologist named Joseph Barrell discovered the presence of **specific gravity** anomalies over Earth's land surfaces that led him to hypothesize that this effect was a result of the interaction between layers with distinct properties. Over time, other geologists expanded on the concept of lithosphere and asthenosphere. In the 1960s, this concept helped explain the theory of continental drift. The composition of the crustal portion of the lithosphere is divided into two types—

continental crust and oceanic crust. Each type of crust has its own characteristics.

ORIGIN AND EVOLUTION OF THE LITHOSPHERE ICE AGES

About 4.5 billion years ago, our solar system began to form. A vast cloud of dust and debris swirled around the star that is our Sun. This cloud eventually began to coalesce into protoplanets. One of these protoplanets, the third one from the Sun, was destined to become planet Earth. As more and more material became packed together, residual heat, heat from radioactive decay, and heat from compression formed the planet into a molten ball. The heavier elements sank toward the center of the molten ball, while lighter elements rose toward the surface. This stratification led to the distinctive layers that characterize the planet today. Eventually, an early, thin atmosphere formed that consisted of hydrogen, ammonia, and water vapor.

After about 100 to 150 million years, the surface of Earth cooled to form a solid crust. Volcanoes ejected lava as well as water vapor and carbon dioxide. Additional water came from comets that impacted the surface. Earth continued cooling and, after about 750 million years, liquid water on the surface formed the oceans. The atmosphere probably consisted of ammonia, methane, water vapor, carbon dioxide, nitrogen, and smaller amounts of other gases. The atmosphere lacked free oxygen because hydrogen or minerals on the surface would have bonded with it. Volcanic activity was intense and, without an ozone layer, ultraviolet radiation bombarded the planet's surface.

About four billion years ago, the first signs of life appeared. Early life most likely depended on ammonia or hydrogen sulfide in the environment. Through a process called **chemosynthesis**, these early organisms derived energy by breaking chemical bonds. In this way, life progressed until around three billion years ago, when some cells began using sunlight as an energy source to combine carbon dioxide and water. In this process, called photosynthesis, carbon dioxide and water combine to form glucose and oxygen.

Oxygen is a chemically active element. As fast as it was produced by photosynthesis, it bonded with elements on the surface, such as iron. As photosynthetic organisms produced more and more oxygen, the iron-rich rocks reacted with the oxygen until all the exposed iron had bonded with the oxygen. At that point, excess oxygen began to accumulate in the atmosphere.

The accumulation of oxygen created an atmosphere more or less like the current atmosphere. The ozone layer formed, preventing most of the Sun's damaging ultraviolet rays from reaching Earth's surface. This allowed life on Earth to expand out into the open without suffering the effects of ultraviolet radiation. The presence of oxygen in the atmosphere had another effect. Oxygen turned out to be toxic to many of the earliest organisms on Earth. Unable to survive in these new conditions, these earlier organisms retreated to areas around underwater volcanic vents.

The evolution of the atmosphere and the oceans led to the hydrologic cycle. The hydrologic cycle made possible the movement of water from the oceans to the atmosphere and back to the Earth's surface. This movement of water set the stage for many dynamic processes that shape the lithosphere as it exists today.

CHEMICAL COMPOSITION OF THE LITHOSPHERE

The most common chemicals in the Earth's crust exist as oxides. The charts below show the most common elements and the percentages of the most common oxides found in the Earth's crust. Frank Wigglesworth Clarke (1847–1931) was a chemist born in Massachusetts. Clarke is regarded as the father of geochemistry. His work on the composition of Earth's crust in the late 1800s and early 1900s is still regarded as accurate today. With additional sampling and newer analytical methods, his numbers have

TABLE 6.1 **THE 8 COMMON ELEMENTS FOUND IN EARTH'S CRUST**		
ELEMENT NAME	**CHEMICAL SYMBOL**	**AMOUNT FOUND IN EARTH'S CRUST (AS A PERCENTAGE)**
Oxygen	O	46.60
Silicon	Si	27.72
Aluminum	Al	8.13
Iron	Fe	5.00
Calcium	Ca	3.63
Sodium	Na	2.83
Potassium	K	2.59
Magnesium	Mg	2.09

been slightly refined, but remain remarkably close to his original calculations. Clarke's calculation showed that about 47% of Earth's crust consisted of oxygen. The most common oxides are those of silicon, aluminum, iron, calcium, magnesium, potassium, and sodium. Silicon is common in minerals found in both igneous and metamorphic rocks.

TABLE 6.2 **COMMON OXIDES FOUND IN EARTH'S CRUST**		
COMPOUND	**OXIDE**	**PERCENTAGE**
silica	SiO_2	66.62
alumina	Al_2O_3	15.40
lime	CaO	3.59
magnesia	MgO	2.48
sodium oxide	Na_2O	3.27
iron oxide	FeO	5.04
water	H_2O	1.52
titanium oxide	TiO_2	0.64
phosphorus pentoxide	P_2O_5	0.15

Differences in Oceanic and Continental Crust

The crust is the outermost layer of rocks and minerals that make up the solid Earth. The crust is distinguished from the underlying mantle rocks by its composition and lower density. Most of the crust can be classified either as **continental crust** or **oceanic crust**. These two types of crust differ in their average age, composition, thickness, and mode of origin.

Continental crust is, on average, older, more silica-rich, and thicker than oceanic crust. It is also more variable in each of these respects. The oldest parts of the continental crust, known as **shields** or **cratons**, include some rocks that are nearly 4 billion years old. Most of the rest of the continental crust consists of the roots of mountain belts, known as **orogens**, which formed at different stages in Earth history. The average thickness of the continental crust is about 25 miles (40 km), but beneath parts of the Andes and the Himalaya mountain ranges, the crust is more than 43 miles (70 km) thick. Over large areas, however, younger sedimentary rocks cover these orogens. In addition, processes operating at **subduction zones** are still generating new continental crust, so that the materials on the continental crust represent a wide range of ages. At the same time, sediments from erosion build up on the continents. Some of this is deposited on the ocean floor to be recycled into the mantle at some subduction zones. Geologic processes, water, and gases from the atmosphere interact to create a wide array of minerals. Sediments from erosion build up on the continents.

Oceanic crust underlies most of Earth's surface that is covered by the oceans. It has a remarkably uniform composition (about 49% SiO_2) and thickness (mostly 3 to 5 miles, or 6 to 8 km). The ocean floor is the most dynamic part of Earth's surface. As a result, no part of the oceanic crust existing today is more than about 200 million years old. New oceanic crust is constantly being generated by seafloor spreading at areas called mid-oceanic ridges, while other parts of the oceanic crust are being recycled back into the mantle at subduction zones.

In many regions, the oceanic crust is covered by a thin layer of sediment less than a half a mile (1 km) thick. This sediment is composed mainly of clay and the shells of organisms. This sediment layer is thinnest near the mid-oceanic ridges, which is the youngest part of the oceanic crust. This layer of sediments becomes thicker farther away from the ridge.

As the ocean floor spreads, these sediments accumulate and are transported to the subduction zones. At a subduction zone, some of the sediments are scraped off the surface of the oceanic crust and pushed up onto the adjacent plate. This action explains why mountains are often found adjacent to these types of plate boundaries.

PHYSICAL AND CHEMICAL WEATHERING

Weathering is the breaking down of rock by a variety of processes. Weathering takes place throughout the zone in which materials of the lithosphere, hydrosphere, atmosphere, and biosphere interact. This zone extends as far below Earth's surface as air, water, and microscopic organisms can readily penetrate, as deep as hundreds of miles. Rocks in the weathering zone usually contain numerous fractures, cracks, and pores through which water, air, and organisms readily pass. Given enough time, these elements produce major changes in the rock.

Weathering creates a loose layer of broken rock and mineral fragments called **regolith**. Fragments in the regolith range in size from microscopic to many miles across, but all result from the chemical and physical breakdown of **bedrock**. As the particles get smaller and smaller, plants become capable of extending roots into them to extract minerals and other nutrients. At this point, the regolith becomes **soil**.

Soil forms a bridge between the lithosphere and the biosphere because of its mineral and organic components. Earth is the only planet that has true soil. The other rocky bodies in the solar system have a blanket of loose rocky material or regolith, which has sometimes been pulverized to a very fine texture but which lacks humus.

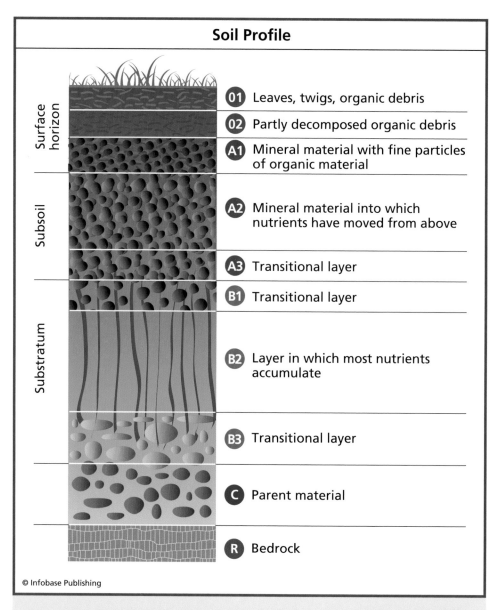

Soil Profile

Surface horizon

O1 Leaves, twigs, organic debris

O2 Partly decomposed organic debris

A1 Mineral material with fine particles of organic material

Subsoil

A2 Mineral material into which nutrients have moved from above

A3 Transitional layer

B1 Transitional layer

Substratum

B2 Layer in which most nutrients accumulate

B3 Transitional layer

C Parent material

R Bedrock

© Infobase Publishing

Figure 6.1   The soil profile is the vertical arrangement of soil down to bedrock. Each division into major horizons are similar in color, texture, structure, reaction, consistency, mineral and chemical composition, and arrangement in the soil profile. Most soils have three major horizons called the surface horizon, the subsoil, and the substratum.

Humus retains some of the chemical nutrients released by decaying organisms and by the chemical weathering of minerals. Humus is critical to soil fertility, which is the ability of a soil to provide nutrients needed by growing plants, such as phosphorus, nitrogen, and potassium. All of the processes that involve living organisms and other soil constituents produce a continuous cycling of plant nutrients between the regolith and the biosphere.

The breakdown processes involved in weathering fall into two categories—**physical weathering** and **chemical weathering**. In physical weathering, rock is broken down into smaller pieces by mechanical processes, but there is no change in its mineral content or chemical composition. Chemical weathering involves dissolution or chemical reactions in the rock, which replace original minerals with new minerals that are stable at Earth's surface. Although physical weathering is distinct from chemical weathering, the two processes almost always occur simultaneously, and their effects are sometimes difficult to separate.

Rocks in the upper half of the crust are brittle. Like any brittle material, rocks break when they are twisted, squeezed, or stretched by tectonic forces. These forces cause fractures and breaks that form **joints** in the bedrock. Joints are the main passageways through which rainwater, air, and small organisms enter the rock, leading to mechanical and chemical weathering.

Physical weathering takes place in four main ways—through freezing of water, formation of crystals, penetration by plant roots, or abrasion. By far the most important type of physical weathering involves the freezing of water.

Most liquids contract when they freeze, and the volume of the resulting solid is less than the volume of the liquid. However, when water freezes, it expands, increasing in volume by about 9%. (For example, a full, capped bottle of water placed in the freezer will burst when the water freezes, because it cannot contain the greater volume of ice.) Wherever temperatures fluctuate around the freezing point for part of the year, water in rocks and soil will alternately freeze and thaw. If the water gets inside a joint in the rock, the freeze-thaw cycles act like a lever that pries the rock apart and eventually causes it to shatter. This process is known as **frost wedging.**

As ice forms, crystals grow, and they expand and push on rocks, causing them to break. As plants grow, their roots grow downward to seek water. Over time, the roots increase in size in both length and diameter. If a root grows down through a crack or fracture in the rock, the increase in diameter can push the rock apart. These processes, along with frost wedging, break rocks apart.

Abrasion is the final type of physical weathering. As the name implies, abrasion is the removal of rock material by friction. Wind, moving water, and glaciers may weather rocks by abrasion. Wind and water carry abrasive materials such as sand that can scour a surface. Glaciers, even though they move much more slowly, carry sand, gravel, and even boulders that act like sandpaper on the surface of the rock below. Glaciers tend to abrade rocks into a very fine powder called rock flour, as discussed in Chapter 5.

Chemical weathering is primarily caused by water that is slightly acidic. When acidified rainwater sinks into the regolith and becomes groundwater, it may dissolve carbon dioxide from decaying organic matter, becoming more strongly acidified. Rainwater can also become more strongly acidified by interacting with sulfur and nitrogen compounds in the atmosphere to produce sulfuric and nitric acids. Acid precipitation is stronger than natural rain, which is weakly acidic, and causes accelerated weathering.

Through **dissolution**, some minerals can be completely removed from a rock without leaving a residue. Some common rock-forming minerals, such as calcite (calcium carbonate) and dolomite (calcium magnesium carbonate), dissolve readily in slightly acidified water.

Water can also alter the mineral content of rock without dissolving it. One reaction of special importance in chemical weathering is **ion exchange**. Ions exist both in solutions and in minerals. Ions form when atoms give up or accept electrons. The difference is that ions in minerals are tightly bonded and fixed in a crystal lattice, whereas ions in solutions can move about randomly and take part in chemical reactions. In ion exchange, hydrogen ions (H^+) from acidic water enter and alter a mineral by displacing larger, positively charged ions such as potassium (K^+), sodium (Na^+), and magnesium (Mg^{2+}).

Where do the mineral salts in rock go after they are dissolved or replaced by hydrogen ions? Some of them remain present in the groundwater, which accounts for the taste or hardness of water. Some of them flow out to sea, adding to the ocean's supply of dissolved salts. If the water evaporates, the dissolved minerals can precipitate out as solid evaporates, such as halite and gypsum.

Another very important process of chemical weathering is **oxidation**. Oxidation is a reaction between minerals and oxygen dissolved in water. Iron and manganese in particular are present in many rock-forming minerals. When such minerals undergo chemical weathering, the iron and manganese are freed and immediately oxidize. Oxidized iron forms an insoluble yellowish mineral called limonite, and manganese forms an insoluble black mineral called pyrolusite. Limonite may lose its water to form hematite, a brick-red-colored mineral that gives a distinctive red color to tropical soils.

Solutional and Depositional Chemical Processes

One type of chemical weathering involves dissolving rocks or minerals. When rocks or minerals are dissolved in water, the substances do not disappear. They are still present in the water. Under the right conditions, they may precipitate out of solution. Nowhere are the processes of dissolution and deposition better illustrated than in caves.

A **cave** is a natural opening, usually in rocks, that is large enough for human entry. There are many different types of caves. Caves include lava tubes, ice caves, large cracks, and solutional features. For discussing solutional and depositional processes, this section will focus on solutional caves. Solutional caves usually form in limestone or gypsum. Limestone is composed of calcium carbonate, or calcite ($CaCO_3$), and gypsum is calcium sulfate ($CaSO_4$). Both limestone and gypsum are soluble to some extent by water. Limestone is more common than gypsum. Even though limestone caves form by solution, other physical processes, such as erosion and collapsing, also contribute to cave development.

As raindrops fall, they can absorb carbon dioxide from the atmosphere, forming a weak solution of carbonic acid (H_2CO_3). As water passes through soil, it absorbs even more carbon dioxide. When the acidic water reaches the limestone, it seeps into cracks in the rock. The carbonic acid slowly dissolves the calcium carbonate. The cracks eventually widen enough to form a cave.

The formation of the cave is not the end of the story. If you have ever been in, or seen pictures of, a cave, you have seen that many of them are filled with beautiful formations. Cave formations include stalactites hanging from the ceiling, stalagmites rising from the floor, and flowstone that looks like frozen waterfalls. These cave formation are made of calcite that precipitated out of water. The dissolution and precipitation reactions are at equilibrium. If the concentration of carbon dioxide decreases in the water, calcium carbonate precipitates out of solution. This takes place through a series of related chemical reactions.

Carbon dioxide is removed from the atmosphere by dissolving in water and forming carbonic acid, as follows:

$$CO_2\ (g) + H_2O\ (l) \rightleftharpoons H_2CO_3\ (aq)\ \text{(carbonic acid)}$$

Once dissolved into water, carbon dioxide is converted into either bicarbonate (HCO_3^-) ions or carbonate (CO_3^{-2}) ions, as follows:

$$H_2CO_3\ (aq) \rightleftharpoons HCO_3^-\ (aq) + H^+\ (aq)$$

$$HCO_3^-\ (aq) \rightleftharpoons H^+\ (aq) + CO_3^{-2}\ (aq)$$

$$CaCO_3(s) + H_2CO_3(aq) \rightleftharpoons Ca^{+2}(aq) + 2HCO^-_3\ (aq)$$

Carbonic acid (H_2CO_3) is formed in rainwater by the reaction between water and carbon dioxide: $H_2O\ (l) + CO_2\ (g) \rightleftharpoons H_2CO_3\ (aq)$.

Figure 6.2   Cave formations are the result of calcite that precipitates out of water.

When this reaction takes place, the acidic rainwater percolates through the ground until it reaches limestone formations. Limestone is dissolved by carbonic acid and caves are created. When the resulting calcium bicarbonate solution is exposed to air, the dissolved CO_2 is released into the atmosphere and calcium carbonate precipitates out to form stalactites.

These chemical equilibrium systems are dynamic. If the equilibrium is disturbed, the reaction will favor either the forward or reverse reaction. The change in equilibrium may be brought about in several different ways. Temperature is one of the factors that changes the equilibrium. Carbon dioxide is more soluble in cold water while calcium carbonate precipitates in hot water and is often found near hot springs. This is also the reason why water heaters have problems with calcium carbonate building up on their coils.

PROCESSES IN THE LITHOSPHERE

The processes by which caves form provide an example of the many dynamic processes that take place in the lithosphere. Most of these processes involve water from the hydrosphere and some require gases from the atmosphere. There are even some processes that require input from the biosphere.

Chemical Processes in the Lithosphere

The lithosphere contains all the elements found on Earth. Material making up the lithosphere is eroded and rebuilt through many different processes. The elements and compounds found in the lithosphere are also constantly being subjected to change. Chemical processes determine their shape and composition. The elements and compounds interact in many ways, and these interactions take place under a wide range of conditions.

Minerals are naturally formed chemical compounds. They form through geological processes. They range in composition from pure elements to simple salts to complex compounds. The term *mineral* refers not only to the chemical composition of a substance but also to its structure. While some minerals may have the same chemical composition, they may vary greatly in structure.

MINERAL COMPOSITION AND STRUCTURE

A mineral is any nonliving, naturally occurring, homogeneous solid with a definite chemical composition and a distinctive crystalline structure. Some minerals have a very simple composition of just a single element. Gold is one such mineral. Gold does not readily react with most other substances, so it is rather common to find it in an elemental form. Silver, on the other hand, is very reactive and is almost never found in its elemental form. Silver readily reacts with other substances and is usually found combined with sulfur, arsenic, antimony, or chlorine. Some minerals have quite complicated compositions, such as muscovite mica—$KAl_2(AlSi_3O_{10})(OH)_2$.

Inorganic processes usually form minerals. Scientists can simulate the inorganic processes by which many minerals form and make synthetic minerals, such as emeralds and diamonds, which are used for experimental or commercial purposes.

Most minerals crystallize in an orderly, three-dimensional geometric form, giving them definite crystalline structures. A mineral's chemical composition and crystalline structure help determine such physical properties as hardness, color, and cleavage.

Minerals combine with other minerals to form rocks. Granite is a common rock that consists of the minerals feldspar, quartz, mica, and amphibole in varying ratios. Rocks are distinguished from minerals by their heterogeneous composition of different minerals.

Mineral Formation

Minerals form from solutions, molten materials, and gases. When a substance is a liquid or gas, its atoms are randomly arranged with no internal structure. When a substance changes from a liquid to a solid or a gas to a solid, its atoms become more and more organized and structured. This organized structure is called a crystal. Some minerals are called gemstones. A gemstone is a mineral or rock that is considered precious or beautiful. Gemstones are often used in jewelry.

A common way to form a crystal is by evaporation of water. A substance that is dissolved in water has a definite number of atoms. As the volume of water decreases through evaporation, the atoms are forced closer and closer together. When enough water has evaporated, the atoms arrange themselves in a crystalline form. The size of the resultant crystal depends on the rate of evaporation. A slow evaporation rate yields few large crystals, while a quick evaporation rate yields many smaller crystals.

Crystals also form if a solution or a gas is cooled or experiences decreased pressure. In general, hot solutions are able to hold more dissolved substance per unit of solution. When a solution has cooled sufficiently, the atoms of the dissolved material, or solute, begin linking together to form a crystalline substance. The same process takes place with changes in pressure. High pressure allows more individual atoms to exist per unit volume of solution. If the pressure on a solution is decreased, the atoms of solute bond together to form a solid mineral.

Many minerals contain impurities. These impurities can vary and each impurity may cause a different effect on the mineral. Quartz, for example, has the chemical formula SiO_2 and is generally colorless in its pure form. If the quartz has a trace amount of titanium (Ti), a slight pinkish coloration is present. This pinkish-colored quartz is called rose quartz. The amount of titanium relative to the amount of silicon and oxygen is minimal, so the titanium is considered an impurity rather than a change in the chemical composition. Therefore, rose quartz is still considered quartz. The gemstone amethyst is a form of quartz that has a pale to deep purple color caused by the presence of the impurity iron (Fe).

Crystalline structures occur with all types of chemical bonds. Most metals exist in a polycrystalline state of many small crystals.

THE NAICA MINE

The Naica Mine is located in Chihuahua, Mexico. It is used to mine zinc from 200 million-year-old limestone. A chamber found in 1910 was named Cave of the Swords because of swordlike selenite crystals in the chamber that were 6.5 feet (2 m) long. Selenite is a relatively rare form of gypsum. In 2000, another chamber was discovered in the mine that has selenite crystals that are 39 feet (12 m) long and up to 6.5 feet (2 m) in diameter. These selenite crystals were formed from hot, mineral-laden water rising up from deep underground. The temperature in the chamber is 150°F (65°C).

Figure 7.1   Huge selenite crystals in the Naica Mine

Metals may also be amorphous or single-crystal. Ionic-bonded crystals can form upon solidification of salts. These form either from a molten fluid or by precipitation from a solution.

Covalent-bonded crystals are also very common. Examples of covalently bonded crystals are diamond, graphite, and silica. Weak forces, known as Van der Waals forces, sometimes play a role in a crystal structure. These weak forces loosely hold together the sheets in the mineral graphite. Most crystalline materials have a variety of crystallographic defects or flaws. The types and structures of these defects can have a profound effect on the properties of the mineral.

Physical Properties of Minerals

The identity of a mineral can be found in a laboratory, using complex and costly procedures. However, by looking at the physical properties, a geologist can quickly identify many minerals right in the field. Some minerals may look similar but have very different properties. These different specific physical properties help to identify a mineral.

Identification of a mineral by its physical properties requires a number of simple observations and tests. The results of all the tests taken together narrow down the identity of the mineral in question. These tests identify some of the most common minerals with surprising accuracy. Some of the more unusual and uncommon minerals may require further testing to reveal their true identity. The common physical characteristics of minerals that help identify them are luster, color, streak, hardness, breakage patterns, specific gravity, effervescence, magnetism, taste, and smell.

Geology books usually provide charts or keys to identifying minerals based on the tests described here. These physical characteristics are widely used for quick identification of minerals.

Luster

Luster describes the way that light reflects from the surface of a mineral. It is often the first test to be made when identifying

Figure 7.2 A streak of hematite

any mineral. There are two basic types of luster—metallic and non-metallic. A mineral having metallic luster looks like metal and is shiny. Minerals having nonmetallic luster show many subtle differences, but most are dull and can be transparent, translucent, or waxy.

Color

Color is easy to see, but it is not very useful for identifying minerals. Most minerals do not have a specific color. As previously mentioned, small amounts of impurities can drastically change the color of a mineral.

Streak

Streak, which is the color of a mineral in powdered form, is a much more reliable property for identifying minerals than is color. A mineral's streak is produced by scraping the mineral across a piece of unglazed porcelain. This action powders a small amount of the mineral to reveal its real color. For example, a streak test of the mineral chromite, which is black like hundreds of other minerals, produces a chocolate-brown color. This distinguishes chromite from most other black minerals.

Hardness

Hardness does not have anything to do with how easy or difficult it is to break a mineral but rather is the resistance of a mineral to being scratched. Hardness is actually a measure of the bonding strength between a mineral's atoms. The stronger the bonds in a mineral, the more difficult it is to scratch that mineral.

Hardness is measured on a scale called the Moh's Hardness Scale, which is based on the relative hardness of one mineral compared to the hardnesses of a group of index minerals. Minerals range in hardness from 1 (very soft) to 10 (very hard). The scale assigns hardness to ten common index minerals, and is based on the ability of one mineral to scratch another. A mineral will scratch any mineral with a lower number but will not scratch a mineral with a higher number. For example, quartz will scratch orthoclase but it will not scratch topaz. Hardness in minerals can vary due to impurities, but is usually definitive.

TABLE 7.1 MOH'S HARDNESS SCALE

HARDNESS	MINERAL	CHEMICAL FORMULA
10	Diamond	C (pure carbon)
9	Corundum	Al_2O_3
8	Topaz	$Al_2SiO_4(OH,F)_2$
7	Quartz	SiO_2
6	Orthoclase	$KAISi_3O_8$
5	Apatite	$Ca_5(PO_4)_3(OH,Cl,F)$
4	Fluorite	CaF_2
3	Calcite	$CaCO_3$
2	Gypsum	$CaSO_4 \cdot 2H_2O$
1	Talc	$Mg_3Si_4O_{10}(OH)_2$

Geologists usually do not carry a set of index minerals for the hardness scale. Instead, they use the hardness of many common items to quickly check a mineral in the field. For example, a fingernail has a hardness of about 2.5. Scratching a mineral with a fingernail can differentiate between gypsum and calcite. A penny has a hardness of 3.5. A knife blade has a hardness of about 4.5, depending on its quality. Common window glass has a hardness of 5.5. Many geologists, however, prefer to carry around a piece of quartz because it has a hardness of 7. Using these common materials, a geologist can get a quick idea of the hardness of an unknown mineral picked up in the field.

Breakage Pattern

The way a mineral breaks is determined by its internal structure. The breakage pattern reveals much about the crystalline structure, so it is almost always a good diagnostic test. However, this test is often difficult to perform in the field. Breakage patterns are divided into two separate categories—fracture and cleavage. Fracture describes the way that a mineral breaks and leaves an uneven surface. Cleavage describes how a mineral splits along parallel planes, leaving one or more smooth surfaces.

Minerals can have 1, 2, 3, 4, or 6 planes of cleavage. If the cleavage has more than one plane, the angle between the planes is also important. Cleavage is often difficult to accurately determine in the field. Also, because it is a destructive test, it is used sparingly.

Specific Gravity

Specific gravity is the weight of a specific volume of a mineral divided by the weight of an equal volume of water at 39°F (4°C) because the specific gravity of pure water is always 1.0, the same value as its density. Specific gravity does not have any units, however, and is usually not measured in the field, although an estimate is useful.

Effervescence

Minerals containing calcium carbonate ($CaCO_3$) will generally react when exposed to acid such as hydrochloric acid (HCl). When acid is dropped onto calcium carbonate, carbon dioxide (CO_2) is released, producing bubbles on the surface of the mineral. Other carbonate-containing minerals may also bubble slightly when acid is applied.

Magnetism

Magnetism is tested with a small piece of ferrous metal, such as a paperclip, or with a compass. Magnetite is a naturally magnetic mineral. It will attract a metal paper clip or deflect the needle of a compass.

Taste and Smell

Some minerals have a distinctive taste or smell. Halite is the mineral sodium chloride (NaCl), or table salt. Other minerals such as sulfur have a distinctive smell. Tests using taste and smell are not widely used and can be dangerous with some minerals.

Rock-Forming Minerals

Minerals are classified by their chemical composition. They are often categorized by their anion, or negative ion. Minerals are inorganic solids with a specific chemical composition and a characteristic regular, geometric arrangement of their constituent atoms. Minerals are divided into distinct groups based upon a similar atomic structure or chemical composition.

Many minerals contain elements that are freely exchanged with other elements that have similar chemical properties through ion exchange. These elements occur as either major elements in the structure of a mineral or as trace elements. Because the substituted ions have similar chemical properties to the ions replaced, the mineral is not usually affected by ionic substitution.

The mineral groups described here are the common groups of minerals. Most minerals fall into one of these categories. There are a number of other types of minerals that are not as common. Many of these minerals are easily refined through oxidation or reduction reactions to obtain metals.

Silicates

Silicates are minerals composed mainly of silicon and oxygen. They are the largest group of minerals and make up more than 95% of all rocks. Some important rock-forming silicates include the feldspars, quartz, olivines, garnets, and micas.

Carbonates

Carbonate minerals contain the carbonate anion (CO_3^{2-}). This group includes calcite (calcium carbonate), dolomite (magnesium/calcium carbonate), and siderite (iron carbonate). Carbonates are commonly deposited on the ocean floor as the shells of dead organisms settle and accumulate. Carbonates are also found in places where evaporation rates are high. They are also found in caves where cave formations form from calcite. Aragonite is another mineral that contains only calcium carbonate. Aragonite is distinguished from calcite by its different crystalline structures.

Sulfates

Sulfates are minerals that contain the sulfate anion (SO_4^{2-}). Sulfates often form where highly saline waters slowly evaporate. This action allows for the formation of both sulfates and halides. Sulfates also occur in hydrothermal systems as sulfide minerals. Another occurrence is as oxidation products of original sulfide minerals. Common sulfate minerals include anhydrite (calcium sulfate), celestine (strontium sulfate), barite (barium sulfate), and gypsum (hydrated calcium sulfate).

Halides

The halides include the fluoride, chloride, and iodide minerals. Halides contain natural salts composed of a metal and a halogen group. Common halides include fluorite (calcium fluoride), halite (sodium chloride), sylvite (potassium chloride), and sal ammoniac (ammonium chloride). Halides are commonly found in evaporation deposits.

Oxides

Oxides are minerals that contain a metal and oxygen. They are important in mining because they form **ores** from which valuable metals can be extracted. Oxides commonly form close to the Earth's surface. They form when minerals undergo chemical weathering involving oxygen in the atmosphere. Common oxides include hematite (iron oxide), magnetite (iron oxide), chromite (iron chromium oxide), and ice (hydrogen oxide). Oxides also include the hydroxide minerals.

Sulfides

Sulfide minerals contain a metal and a sulfide ion (S^{2-}). Many sulfide minerals are economically important as metal ores. Common sulfides include pyrite (iron sulfide), chalcopyrite (copper iron sulfide), and galena (lead sulfide).

Phosphates

The phosphates include any mineral with a tetrahedral crystal in the form of AO_4, where A can be phosphorus, antimony, arsenic, or vanadium. Phosphate is the most common. Apatite is an important biological mineral found in teeth and bones of many animals.

Native Elements

The native elements include metals such as gold, silver, and copper, and semimetals and nonmetals such as antimony, bismuth, graphite, and sulfur.

PETROLEUM, NATURAL GAS, AND COAL FORMATION

Petroleum, which is also called crude oil, is a naturally occurring liquid mixture of hydrocarbons. Petroleum is usually black or dark brown in color. The hydrocarbons exist as chains of varying length and are mainly alkanes. Alkanes are saturated chains of single-bonded carbon atoms and hydrogen atoms. Petroleum may also contain small amounts of nonmetallic elements such as sulfur, oxygen, and nitrogen.

Petroleum is used primarily in the production of fuels, such as heating oil, diesel, and gasoline. These are energy-rich fuels and are used to power cars, trucks, planes, and ships and to provide fuel for heating. Petroleum-based fuels are ideal for these purposes because they are easy to transport and petroleum is relatively abundant.

Petroleum forms when ancient organic material is heated and compressed over time. This process breaks the organic material down into kerogen, a waxy organic material. With more heat and pressure, the kerogen becomes liquid petroleum. Petroleum seeps through rocks in the crust until it is trapped by geologic structures from where it can be tapped and pumped out.

Natural gas is often associated with petroleum. Natural gas is primarily methane but may contain trace amounts of ethane, butane, helium, and hydrogen. Natural gas is often found associated with petroleum fields and coal beds. It is used mainly for heating, cooking, and energy production. Because it is a gas, it is distributed through pipes. Methane is odorless. During processing, a chemical called mercaptan is added to give it an odor that can be detected in case of a leak.

Natural gas forms in much the same way as petroleum. The hydrocarbon chains sometimes break down, however, to form methane, the simplest hydrocarbon. Methane gas also migrates through the rocks in the crust and is trapped by geologic structures. When these structures are tapped, the methane gas flows out of the well under pressure.

Coal is a fossil fuel that forms from decaying plant materials. It is a combustible brownish-black rock composed mainly of carbon. Coal forms as a sedimentary rock when dead organic plant material is buried, compressed, and lithified. Coal is divided into three classes based on its hardness. Anthracite is the hardest and cleanest-burning type of coal. Bituminous coal is dense, but it is not as hard as anthracite. Lignite, commonly called brown coal, is the lowest grade of coal. Coal is mainly used to produce heat and energy.

Petroleum, natural gas, and coal are all commonly used as energy sources. Because each of these is formed from ancient organic material, they are called fossil fuels. Fossil fuels are part of the carbon cycle. These fuels represent carbon that was removed from the carbon cycle millions of years ago. The storing, or sequestering, of carbon for long periods of time removes excess carbon from the carbon cycle. When fossil fuels are burned as an energy source, the sequestered carbon is released back into the environment as carbon dioxide. The injection of this previously sequestered carbon is increasing the levels of carbon dioxide in the atmosphere. Because carbon dioxide is a greenhouse gas, this may well be affecting the global climate.

ADDRESSING THE HYDROSPHERE

The lithosphere is connected to the hydrosphere and the atmosphere in many different ways. Both the atmosphere and the hydrosphere influence and contribute to the chemical processes that take place in the lithosphere. In the preceding chapters, the interconnections among the atmosphere, hydrosphere, and lithosphere have been explored. The connections to the biosphere have been mentioned but not fully explored. The next chapter describes the influence of the biosphere on the atmosphere, hydrosphere, and lithosphere.

Biosphere

Russian scientist Vladimir Vernadsky coined the term biosphere in the 1920s. The biosphere is the life zone of Earth. It is made up of all living organisms and all organic matter that has not yet decomposed. (Evidence indicates that life on Earth began between 4.5 and 3.8 billion years ago.) The biosphere makes Earth different from all other planets in the solar system.

Living organisms facilitate chemical reactions such as photosynthesis-respiration and carbonate precipitation. These reactions have had a profound effect on the chemical composition of Earth's atmosphere. Photosynthesis transformed the atmosphere from a reducing environment to an oxidizing environment containing free oxygen.

During photosynthesis, energy and matter pass from the environment to plants. When animals eat plants, energy and matter is passed on to the animals. When one animal eats another animal,

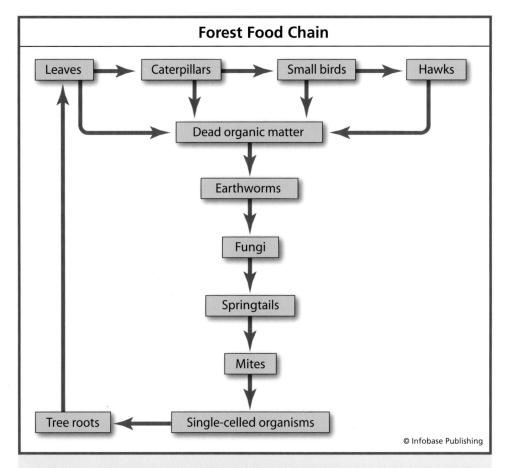

Figure 8.1   A typical forest food chain has many different steps and involves many different organisms. A food chain also shows the flow of energy and organic matter from one organism to the next.

the energy contained in the first animal is also passed on. This flow of matter and energy is called a **food chain**.

The first tier of a food chain is made up of the primary producers that are capable of photosynthesis. The primary producers convert matter into a form that is usable by other organisms. When producers are eaten, this energy and matter is transferred to the next step in the food chain. Energy and matter is transferred from one level of the food chain to the next with an efficiency of about 10%. This means that each tier of the food chain becomes smaller as there is less energy and matter available.

Not all of the matter passed along the food chain is useful to organisms. For example, mercury is a heavy metal and a pollutant. Plants can absorb mercury from the soil. When the plant is eaten, the mercury is passed to the animal that eats the plant. If that animal is eaten, the mercury is then passed to the consuming animal. Over time, this type of matter builds up, or accumulates, in organisms as they continue to consume other contaminated organisms.

BIOACCUMULATION

Bioaccumulation is a general term for the accumulation of substances, such as pesticides, metals, or other chemicals, in an organism. Bioaccumulation occurs when the rate of intake for a substance exceeds the rate at which the substance is released back into the environment. The accumulation process involves the biological sequestering of substances that enter the organism through respiration, food intake, skin contact with the substance, or other means. This process results in an organism having a concentration of the substance that is higher than its concentration in the organism's surrounding environment.

The level at which a given substance is bioaccumulated depends on many factors. The rate of intake of the substance is a controlling factor. If large amounts of a substance are taken in rapidly, they will accumulate. However, a small amount of a substance taken in over a long period of time may also accumulate. The rate at which the substance is removed from the body is another controlling factor. Some substances, such as organic pesticides, are soluble in fats. When these substances enter the body of an animal, they dissolve in the animal's fat cells. The pesticide remains in the fat cells until the fat is metabolized. If another animal eats the organism, the pesticide is passed to the consuming organism. If an animal

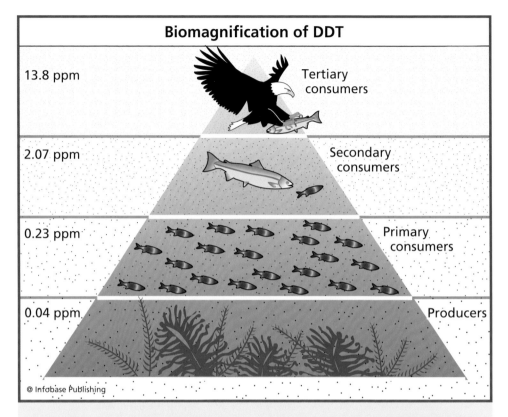

Figure 8.2   This diagram shows that at each successive feeding level, the concentration of DDT greatly increases. Those animals at the top of the food chain accumulate more DDT than the organisms below.

eats many other animals containing the pesticide, it takes in much larger amounts of the pesticide.

Biomagnification is the bioaccumulation of a substance up the food chain. Biomagnification occurs by transfer of residues of the substance in smaller organisms that are eaten by larger organisms in the chain. This process results in higher concentrations of certain substances in organisms at higher levels in the food chain. Biomagnification can result in higher concentrations of the substance than would be expected due only to exposure in the environment.

Bioaccumulation and biomagnification are real problems for humans. Humans eat foods from all levels of the food chain. As a result, it is possible for humans to ingest rather high doses of toxins that have become bioaccumulated and biomagnified in their food. Fish tend to have rather long food chains, so it is possible for toxins to biomagnify rapidly in fish. Tuna, for example, are at the top of their food chain, so they are likely to biomagnify environmental toxins.

BIOGEOCHEMICAL CYCLES

Earth is essentially a closed system for matter. All the elements needed for the Earth's structure and its chemical processes come from the elements that were present in the crust when it was formed billions of years ago. This matter continually cycles through Earth's atmosphere, hydrosphere, lithosphere, and biosphere. Different elements cycle through at different rates. Some take only a few days, while others take millions of years. These cycles are called **biogeochemical cycles** because they include a variety of biological, geological, and chemical processes.

Many elements pass through these cycles. Some are trace elements, while others are critical to life. Elements critical for life include carbon, nitrogen, oxygen, hydrogen, sulfur, and phosphorous. Because all living organisms need these elements, they must be available. Carbon is relatively rare in the Earth's crust. Nitrogen, though abundant in the atmosphere, is present in a form that is not readily usable by living organisms.

The biogeochemical cycles transport, store, and make available these important elements. Each biogeochemical cycle follows many different pathways. Some molecules may cycle very quickly depending on the pathway. Conversely, carbon atoms in deep ocean sediments may take hundreds to millions of years to cycle completely through the system. An average water molecule resides in the atmosphere for about ten days, although it may be transported many miles before it returns to Earth's surface as rain.

The rate at which a substance cycles depends on its chemical reactivity and its physical state. Gas molecules are transported quickly. On the other hand, phosphorous has no gaseous phase and is relatively inactive. It moves very slowly through its cycle. Phosphorous is stored in large amounts in sediments on the ocean floor or in Earth's crust, and is recycled back to the surface only over very long periods of time through upwelling of ocean waters or weathering of rocks.

Carbon Cycle

Carbon is another compound that passes through a biogeochemical cycle. All living organisms are made up of carbon compounds. All the carbon found in an organism comes from the environment. The source of carbon for living organisms is the atmosphere. The atmosphere only contains about 0.038% carbon dioxide. However, this seemingly small amount is very important.

Plants take in carbon dioxide during photosynthesis and use it to build organic carbon molecules. In photosynthesis, plants combine carbon dioxide and water and use energy from the Sun to make glucose. Plants then convert glucose into other compounds and store it for later use. When animals eat plants, they take in the stored energy and use it to build tissues. This process transfers carbon from plants to animals.

Plants and animals break down carbon compounds during cellular respiration. This process releases both stored energy and carbon dioxide, which is returned to the atmosphere. When plants such as trees grow, they tie up carbon in their tissues. When they burn, the carbon is released back into the environment as carbon compounds—mainly carbon dioxide. These are only two of the ways that carbon is returned to the atmosphere as carbon dioxide, however.

When plants and animals die, they decompose, or break down. Decomposition releases carbon directly backs into the atmosphere. Sometimes, the remains of plants or animals are buried quickly or decompose in swamps or bogs with low oxygen levels.

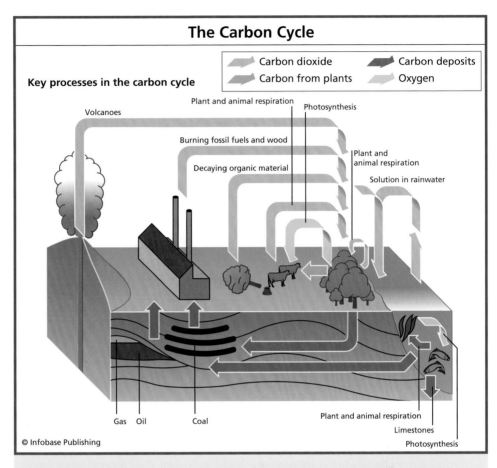

The Carbon Cycle

Key processes in the carbon cycle

Carbon dioxide
Carbon from plants
Carbon deposits
Oxygen

Volcanoes
Plant and animal respiration
Photosynthesis
Burning fossil fuels and wood
Plant and animal respiration
Decaying organic material
Solution in rainwater

Gas   Oil   Coal
Plant and animal respiration
Limestones
Photosynthesis

© Infobase Publishing

Figure 8.3   Carbon is cycled through the atmosphere, hydrosphere, lithosphere, and biosphere. Carbon is important to all living organisms and required for many chemical processes. This diagram shows how carbon is cycled through Earth.

In such cases, the carbon is tied up and prevented from immediately returning to the atmosphere. In fact, the carbon may be locked away for thousands or millions of years. Geological processes, heat, and pressure may turn this trapped carbon into fossil fuels—oil, coal, or natural gas. When these fossil fuels are burned for energy, the carbon is released back into the atmosphere as carbon dioxide.

The formation of fossil fuels is not the only way carbon becomes tied up. Large amounts of carbon dioxide are dissolved in the oceans. Some marine organisms convert this carbon dioxide into calcium carbonate for their shells. When these organisms die, their shells fall to the bottom of the ocean. In some oceans, chemical processes cause carbon dioxide dissolved in ocean water to form calcium carbonate and precipitate, or settle out. Given enough time, the shells and calcium carbonate build up and turn into limestone. This process may tie up carbon for millions of years.

The carbon cycle maintains a delicate balance between carbon in the atmosphere and carbon that is tied up in organisms or the environment. This balance is altered when fossil fuels are burned. Exactly how this will affect the carbon balance is debated among scientists.

Nitrogen Cycle

The nitrogen cycle starts with elemental nitrogen in the air, which makes up 78.1% of the atmosphere. Nitrogen reacts with oxygen in the air to form nitrogen oxide. Nitrogen only reacts with oxygen under conditions of high temperature and pressure found near lightning bolts and in combustion reactions in power plants or internal combustion engines.

Two different oxides of nitrogen are found in the air: nitric oxide (NO) and nitrogen dioxide (NO_2). Nitrogen dioxide eventually reacts with water in raindrops to form nitric acid (HNO_3). This is one type of acid precipitation.

Nitrogen in the air becomes available to plants and animals mostly through the actions of bacteria and algae in a process known as **nitrogen fixation**. Nodules form on the roots of legume plants, such as clover, alfalfa, and soybeans. It is in these nodules that nitrogen-fixing bacteria convert nitrogen from the air into ammonia (NH_3). The ammonia is oxidized by other bacteria first into nitrite ions (NO_2^-) and then into nitrate ions (NO_3^-). Plants utilize the nitrate ions as a nutrient or fertilizer. Nitrogen is incorporated into many amino acids, which are building blocks used to make proteins.

To complete the nitrogen cycle, other bacteria in the soil carry out a process known as **denitrification**, which converts nitrates back to nitrogen gas. A side product of this reaction is the production of nitrous oxide (N_2O). Nitrous oxide is a greenhouse gas. In fact, nitrous oxide is the number three greenhouse gas behind carbon dioxide and methane. In addition to being a greenhouse gas, nitrous oxide also destroys ozone when it reaches the stratosphere.

Phosphorus Cycle

Unlike the most compounds found in biogeochemical cycles, phosphorus is not found in the atmosphere because it is usually liquid at normal temperatures and pressures. For this reason, phosphorus is confined to the lithosphere, atmosphere, and biosphere.

Phosphorus moves very slowly from deposits on land and in ocean-floor sediments, to living organisms, and then much more slowly back into the soil and water. The phosphorus cycle is the slowest of the matter cycles. However, phosphorus is very important to plants and animals.

In the lithosphere, phosphorus is commonly found in rocks and ocean sediments as phosphate salts. Phosphate salts from weathered rocks dissolve slightly in water and will be absorbed by plants. Phosphorus in soil is usually found in very low concentrations, so it is often the limiting factor for plant growth. Phosphorus is a key ingredient in fertilizers used on agricultural crops to boost yield. Phosphates are also limiting factors for plant growth in rivers, lakes, and streams because phosphate salts are not very water-soluble. Phosphate salts are passed from plants to animals when the plants are consumed.

The cycling of phosphorus through plants and animals is much faster than the cycling of phosphorus from rocks and sediments into plants. When animals and plants die, phosphates return to the environment during decay. After that, phosphorus either ends up in sediments or is recycled into plants. If the phosphorus ends up in the sediments, it will eventually be released again through weathering, and the cycle continues.

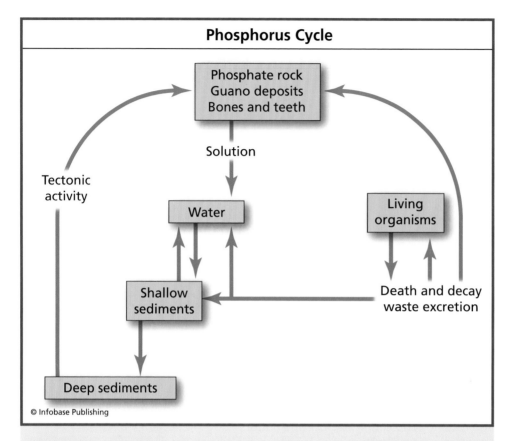

Figure 8.4   Phosphorus is an important element for both plants and animals. Phosphorus is cycled through living organisms, the hydrosphere, and the lithosphere.

ENERGY SOURCES

All organisms need energy to carry out their biological processes. Humans also need energy to power their civilizations. Energy is needed for transportation, manufacturing, and raising food. Humans are the only organisms capable of drastically altering their environment. The production of energy has changed Earth in many ways. Humans depend on fossil fuels for much of their energy production. Burning these fuels releases carbon that has been sequestered for millions of years. This action is causing carbon dioxide in the atmosphere to reach a level that is higher than it has been in more than 650,000 years. It is likely that the increased carbon dioxide levels will affect the global climate.

Since about 1850, in the wake of the Industrial Revolution, world energy consumption has been rising steadily. Coal was the main energy source in the eighteenth and nineteenth centuries. It was used for heating and transportation. Coal-fired steamships replaced sailing ships. Trains powered by coal-fired steam engines carried goods and supplies over long distances. Coal is still used for energy production in many areas. Coal-burning power plants produce oxides of sulfur and nitrogen that contribute to acid precipitation.

Beginning in the early twentieth century, petroleum was processed into gasoline and diesel oil for fuel. Fuel oil replaced coal as an energy source on ships and was used for heating homes. Today, transportation on land and in the air requires vast amounts of energy from fossil fuels. The increased use of fossil fuels has resulted in the release of more carbon dioxide into the environment.

Fossil fuels are examples of **nonrenewable energy sources**. Nonrenewable energy sources are ones that, once used, are no longer available. The processes that produce fossil fuels take millions of years to complete. Humans are using fossil fuels at an ever-increasing rate, faster than these fuels can be replaced. It is certain that at some point, the demand will exceed the supply. Once the supply is used up, it will not be replaced in thousands of lifetimes.

As the term suggests, **renewable energy sources** are those that are readily replaced. Such resources are unlimited in the amount of energy they provide. The initial cost of harnessing such renewable energy sources as wind, solar, geothermal, and hydroelectric can be expensive. But once established, they provide cheap energy. Unfortunately, renewable energy sources are able to meet only some of our energy needs.

The big advantage of renewable energy sources is that they do not produce environmentally harmful materials, such as carbon dioxide, as they generate power. By replacing a percentage of our fossil fuel use with renewable energy sources, the amounts of carbon dioxide, sulfur dioxide, and nitrogen oxides released into the environment would be greatly reduced.

Nuclear energy is a nonrenewable energy source because, like fossil fuels, nuclear fuel—uranium—is nonrenewable. The isotope uranium-235 (U-235) is not common. Uranium-238 (U-238), however, is plentiful. It makes up about 99% of all the uranium on Earth, while U-235 only makes up about 0.7%.

In a nuclear reactor, the concentration of U-235 must be 2% to 3%. Fortunately, U-238 can be enriched or refined to increase the concentration of U-235.

In a nuclear reactor, uranium nuclei are split, releasing tremendous amounts of energy. Albert Einstein developed the mathematical formula that explains this conversion of matter to energy in the following equation:

$$E = mc^2$$

According to the equation:

Energy [E] equals mass [m] multiplied by the
speed of light squared [c^2]

The splitting of an atom is called nuclear fission. The energy released during a fission reaction is in the form of both heat and light energy. This energy, when released slowly, can be harnessed to generate electricity. When it is released all at once, a tremendous explosion results, as in a nuclear bomb.

In a nuclear power plant, U-235 is used as fuel. It is processed into tiny pellets that are loaded into long rods that are inserted into the nuclear reactor. The pellets are then bombarded by neutrons, causing nuclear fission to take place in a controlled chain reaction. During a chain reaction, additional neutrons released by the splitting of the U-235 atoms strike other uranium atoms, causing them to split and release more neutrons. Control rods are used to absorb some of the neutrons, keeping the chain reaction from proceeding too fast.

This chain reaction releases tremendous amounts of thermal energy. This energy is transferred as heat to a boiler where it is used to heat water. The heated water from around the nuclear core is sent to a heat exchanger. The heat exchanger takes heat from the reactor water and changes it to steam. The steam then turns a turbine to generate electricity.

A nuclear reaction also creates radioactive waste. The radioactive material is a solid, and it is shielded to make sure it does not spill. This radioactive material is very toxic and dangerous. It must be stored where it will not leak or enter the environment. This material remains radioactive for tens of thousands of years. Storage of radioactive waste is one of the biggest concerns about nuclear power.

CONNECTING THE SYSTEMS

Throughout this book, the interactions among the lithosphere, atmosphere, hydrosphere, and biosphere have been described. All four of these systems are interconnected. When something happens in one system, the effects on the other systems can be far reaching. These systems act in balance with each other and maintain an equilibrium. When a change occurs in one system, a new equilibrium is created. Humans are the only organism on Earth that has the ability to affect all four of the systems. Human actions bring about many changes to each of the systems.

PERIODIC TABLE OF THE ELEMENTS

Legend:
- 3 — Atomic number
- Li — Symbol
- 6.941 — Atomic mass

1 IA	2 IIA	3 IIIB	4 IVB	5 VB	6 VIB	7 VIIB	8 VIIIB	9 VIIIB
1 H 1.00794								
3 Li 6.941	4 Be 9.0122							
11 Na 22.9898	12 Mg 24.3051							
19 K 39.0938	20 Ca 40.078	21 Sc 44.9559	22 Ti 47.867	23 V 50.9415	24 Cr 51.9962	25 Mn 54.938	26 Fe 55.845	27 Co 58.9332
37 Rb 85.4678	38 Sr 87.62	39 Y 88.906	40 Zr 91.224	41 Nb 92.9064	42 Mo 95.94	43 Tc (98)	44 Ru 101.07	45 Rh 102.9055
55 Cs 132.9054	56 Ba 137.328	57-70 ☆	71 Lu 174.967	72 Hf 178.49	73 Ta 180.948	74 W 183.84	75 Re 186.207	76 Os 190.23	77 Ir 192.217
87 Fr (223)	88 Ra (226)	89-102 ★	103 Lr (260)	104 Rf (261)	105 Db (262)	106 Sg (266)	107 Bh (262)	108 Hs (263)	109 Mt (268)

☆ Lanthanoids

★ Actinoids

57 La 138.9055	58 Ce 140.115	59 Pr 140.908	60 Nd 144.24	61 Pm (145)
89 Ac (227)	90 Th 232.0381	91 Pa 231.036	92 U 238.0289	93 Np (237)

Numbers in parentheses are atomic mass numbers of most stable isotopes.

			Metals

			Non-metals

			Metalloids

			Unknown

							18 VIIIA
		13 IIIA	14 IVA	15 VA	16 VIA	17 VIIA	2 He 4.0026

10 VIIIB	11 IB	12 IIB	5 B 10.81	6 C 12.011	7 N 14.0067	8 O 15.9994	9 F 18.9984	10 Ne 20.1798
			13 Al 26.9815	14 Si 28.0855	15 P 30.9738	16 S 32.067	17 Cl 35.4528	18 Ar 39.948
28 Ni 58.6934	29 Cu 63.546	30 Zn 65.409	31 Ga 69.723	32 Ge 72.61	33 As 74.9216	34 Se 78.96	35 Br 79.904	36 Kr 83.798
46 Pd 106.42	47 Ag 107.8682	48 Cd 112.412	49 In 114.818	50 Sn 118.711	51 Sb 121.760	52 Te 127.60	53 I 126.9045	54 Xe 131.29
78 Pt 195.08	79 Au 196.9655	80 Hg 200.59	81 Tl 204.3833	82 Pb 207.2	83 Bi 208.9804	84 Po (209)	85 At (210)	86 Rn (222)
110 Ds (271)	111 Rg (272)	112 Uub (277)	113 Uut (284)	114 Uuq (285)	115 Uup (288)	116 Uuh (292)	117 Uus ?	118 Uuo ?

62 Sm 150.36	63 Eu 151.966	64 Gd 157.25	65 Tb 158.9253	66 Dy 162.500	67 Ho 164.9303	68 Er 167.26	69 Tm 168.9342	70 Yb 173.04
94 Pu (244)	95 Am 243	96 Cm (247)	97 Bk (247)	98 Cf (251)	99 Es (252)	100 Fm (257)	101 Md (258)	102 No (259)

ELECTRON CONFIGURATIONS

1
IA
ns^1

1 H $1s^1$	2 ns^2

Atomic number

3 Li — Symbol

[He] $2s^1$ — Electron configuration

3 Li [He]$2s^1$	4 Be [He]$2s^2$

11 Na [Ne]$3s^1$	12 Mg [Ne]$3s^2$

		3 IIIB	**4** IVB	**5** VB	**6** VIB	**7** VIIB	**8** VIIIB	**9** VIIIB
19 K [Ar]$4s^1$	20 Ca [Ar]$4s^2$	21 Sc [Ar]$4s^23d^1$	22 Ti [Ar]$4s^23d^2$	23 V [Ar]$4s^23d^3$	24 Cr [Ar]$4s^13d^5$	25 Mn [Ar]$4s^23d^5$	26 Fe [Ar]$4s^23d^6$	27 Co [Ar]$4s^23d^7$
37 Rb [Kr]$5s^1$	38 Sr [Kr]$5s^2$	39 Y [Kr]$5s^24d^1$	40 Zr [Kr]$5s^24d^2$	41 Nb [Kr]$5s^14d^4$	42 Mo [Kr]$5s^14d^5$	43 Tc [Kr]$5s^14d^6$	44 Ru [Kr]$5s^14d^7$	45 Rh [Kr]$5s^14d^8$
55 Cs [Xe]$6s^1$	56 Ba [Xe]$6s^2$	57-70 ☆	71 Lu [Xe]$6s^24f^{14}5d^1$	72 Hf [Xe]$4f^{14}6s^25d^2$	73 Ta [Xe]$6s^25d^3$	74 W [Xe]$6s^25d^4$	75 Re [Xe]$6s^25d^5$	76 Os [Xe]$6s^25d^6$	77 Ir [Xe]$6s^25d^7$
87 Fr [Rn]$7s^1$	88 Ra [Rn]$7s^2$	89-102 ★	103 Lr [Rn]$7s^25f^{14}6d^1$	104 Rf [Rn]$7s^26d^2$	105 Db [Rn]$7s^26d^3$	106 Sg [Rn]$7s^26d^4$	107 Bh [Rn]$7s^26d^5$	108 Hs [Rn]$7s^26d^6$	109 Mt [Rn]$7s^26d^7$

☆ Lanthanoids

★ Actinoids

57 La [Xe] $6s^25d^1$	58 Ce [Xe] $6s^24f^15d^1$	59 Pr [Xe] $6s^24f^35d^0$	60 Nd [Xe] $6s^24f^45d^0$	61 Pm [Xe] $6s^24f^55d^0$
89 Ac [Rn]$7s^26d^1$	90 Th [Rn] $7s^25f^06d^2$	91 Pa [Rn] $7s^25f^26d^1$	92 U [Rn] $7s^25f^36d^1$	93 Np [Rn] $7s^25f^46d^1$

			18
			VIIIA
			ns^2np^6

13	14	15	16	17	2 He
IIIA	IVA	VA	VIA	VIIA	
ns^2np^1	ns^2np^2	ns^2np^3	ns^2np^4	ns^2np^5	$1s^2$

10	11	12	13	14	15	16	17	18
VIIIB	IB	IIB						
			5 B	6 C	7 N	8 O	9 F	10 Ne
			$[He]2s^22p^1$	$[He]2s^22p^2$	$[He]2s^22p^3$	$[He]2s^22p^4$	$[He]2s^22p^5$	$[He]2s^22p^6$
			13 Al	14 Si	15 P	16 S	17 Cl	18 Ar
			$[Ne]3s^23p^1$	$[Ne]3s^23p^2$	$[Ne]3s^23p^3$	$[Ne]3s^23p^4$	$[Ne]3s^23p^5$	$[Ne]3s^23p^6$
28 Ni	29 Cu	30 Zn	31 Ga	32 Ge	33 As	34 Se	35 Br	36 Kr
$[Ar]4s^23d^8$	$[Ar]4s^13d^{10}$	$[Ar]4s^23d^{10}$	$[Ar]4s^24p^1$	$[Ar]4s^24p^2$	$[Ar]4s^24p^3$	$[Ar]4s^24p^4$	$[Ar]4s^24p^5$	$[Ar]4s^24p^6$
46 Pd	47 Ag	48 Cd	49 In	50 Sn	51 Sb	52 Te	53 I	54 Xe
$[Kr]4d^{10}$	$[Kr]5s^14d^{10}$	$[Kr]5s^24d^{10}$	$[Kr]5s^25p^1$	$[Kr]5s^25p^2$	$[Kr]5s^25p^3$	$[Kr]5s^25p^4$	$[Kr]5s^25p^5$	$[Kr]5s^25p^6$
78 Pt	79 Au	80 Hg	81 Tl	82 Pb	83 Bi	84 Po	85 At	86 Rn
$[Xe]6s^15d^9$	$[Xe]6s^15d^{10}$	$[Xe]6s^25d^{10}$	$[Xe]6s^26p^1$	$[Xe]6s^26p^2$	$[Xe]6s^26p^3$	$[Xe]6s^26p^4$	$[Xe]6s^26p^5$	$[Xe]6s^26p^6$
110 Ds	111 Rg	112 Uub	113 Uut	114 Uuq	115 Uup	116 Uuh	117 Uus	118 Uuo
$[Rn]7s^16d^9$	$[Rn]7s^16d^{10}$	$[Rn]7s^26d^{10}$	?	?	?	?	?	?

62 Sm	63 Eu	64 Gd	65 Tb	66 Dy	67 Ho	68 Er	69 Tm	70 Yb
[Xe]	[Xe]	[Xe]	[Xe]	[Xe]	[Xe]	[Xe]	[Xe]	[Xe]
$6s^24f^65d^0$	$6s^24f^75d^0$	$6s^24f^75d^1$	$6s^24f^95d^0$	$6s^24f^{10}5d^0$	$6s^24f^{11}5d^0$	$6s^24f^{12}5d^0$	$6s^24f^{13}5d^0$	$6s^24f^{14}5d^0$
94 Pu	95 Am	96 Cm	97 Bk	98 Cf	99 Es	100 Fm	101 Md	102 No
[Rn]	[Rn]	[Rn]	[Rn]	[Rn]	[Rn]	[Rn]	[Rn]	[Rn]
$7s^25f^66d^0$	$7s^25f^76d^0$	$7s^25f^76d^1$	$7s^25f^96d^0$	$7s^25f^{10}6d^0$	$7s^25f^{11}6d^0$	$7s^25f^{12}6d^0$	$7s^25f^{13}6d^0$	$7s^25f^{14}6d^1$

TABLE OF ATOMIC MASSES

ELEMENT	SYMBOL	ATOMIC NUMBER	ATOMIC MASS	ELEMENT	SYMBOL	ATOMIC NUMBER	ATOMIC MASS
Actinium	Ac	89	(227)	Francium	Fr	87	(223)
Aluminum	Al	13	26.9815	Gadolinium	Gd	64	157.25
Americium	Am	95	243	Gallium	Ga	31	69.723
Antimony	Sb	51	121.76	Germanium	Ge	32	72.61
Argon	Ar	18	39.948	Gold	Au	79	196.9655
Arsenic	As	33	74.9216	Hafnium	Hf	72	178.49
Astatine	At	85	(210)	Hassium	Hs	108	(263)
Barium	Ba	56	137.328	Helium	He	2	4.0026
Berkelium	Bk	97	(247)	Holmium	Ho	67	164.9303
Beryllium	Be	4	9.0122	Hydrogen	H	1	1.00794
Bismuth	Bi	83	208.9804	Indium	In	49	114.818
Bohrium	Bh	107	(262)	Iodine	I	53	126.9045
Boron	B	5	10.81	Iridium	Ir	77	192.217
Bromine	Br	35	79.904	Iron	Fe	26	55.845
Cadmium	Cd	48	112.412	Krypton	Kr	36	83.798
Calcium	Ca	20	40.078	Lanthanum	La	57	138.9055
Californium	Cf	98	(251)	Lawrencium	Lr	103	(260)
Carbon	C	6	12.011	Lead	Pb	82	207.2
Cerium	Ce	58	140.115	Lithium	Li	3	6.941
Cesium	Cs	55	132.9054	Lutetium	Lu	71	174.967
Chlorine	Cl	17	35.4528	Magnesium	Mg	12	24.3051
Chromium	Cr	24	51.9962	Manganese	Mn	25	54.938
Cobalt	Co	27	58.9332	Meitnerium	Mt	109	(268)
Copper	Cu	29	63.546	Mendelevium	Md	101	(258)
Curium	Cm	96	(247)	Mercury	Hg	80	200.59
Darmstadtium	Ds	110	(271)	Molybdenum	Mo	42	95.94
Dubnium	Db	105	(262)	Neodymium	Nd	60	144.24
Dysprosium	Dy	66	162.5	Neon	Ne	10	20.1798
Einsteinium	Es	99	(252)	Neptunium	Np	93	(237)
Erbium	Er	68	167.26	Nickel	Ni	28	58.6934
Europium	Eu	63	151.966	Niobium	Nb	41	92.9064
Fermium	Fm	100	(257)	Nitrogen	N	7	14.0067
Fluorine	F	9	18.9984	Nobelium	No	102	(259)

ELEMENT	SYMBOL	ATOMIC NUMBER	ATOMIC MASS	ELEMENT	SYMBOL	ATOMIC NUMBER	ATOMIC MASS
Osmium	Os	76	190.23	Silicon	Si	14	28.0855
Oxygen	O	8	15.9994	Silver	Ag	47	107.8682
Palladium	Pd	46	106.42	Sodium	Na	11	22.9898
Phosphorus	P	15	30.9738	Strontium	Sr	38	87.62
Platinum	Pt	78	195.08	Sulfur	S	16	32.067
Plutonium	Pu	94	(244)	Tantalum	Ta	73	180.948
Polonium	Po	84	(209)	Technetium	Tc	43	(98)
Potassium	K	19	39.0938	Tellurium	Te	52	127.6
Praseodymium	Pr	59	140.908	Terbium	Tb	65	158.9253
Promethium	Pm	61	(145)	Thallium	Tl	81	204.3833
Protactinium	Pa	91	231.036	Thorium	Th	90	232.0381
Radium	Ra	88	(226)	Thulium	Tm	69	168.9342
Radon	Rn	86	(222)	Tin	Sn	50	118.711
Rhenium	Re	75	186.207	Titanium	Ti	22	47.867
Rhodium	Rh	45	102.9055	Tungsten	W	74	183.84
Roentgenium	Rg	111	(272)	Ununbium	Uub	112	(277)
Rubidium	Rb	37	85.4678	Uranium	U	92	238.0289
Ruthenium	Ru	44	101.07	Vanadium	V	23	50.9415
Rutherfordium	Rf	104	(261)	Xenon	Xe	54	131.29
Samarium	Sm	62	150.36	Ytterbium	Yb	70	173.04
Scandium	Sc	21	44.9559	Yttrium	Y	39	88.906
Seaborgium	Sg	106	(266)	Zinc	Zn	30	65.409
Selenium	Se	34	78.96	Zirconium	Zr	40	91.224

GLOSSARY

Acid rain   Precipitation with a lowered pH that results from gases such as sulfur dioxide and nitrogen dioxide dissolving into the precipitation; also called acid precipitation.

Acid/acidic   A substance that has a pH lower than 7 due to an excess of hydronium ions.

Adhesive forces   Forces that hold water molecules together.

Aerosol   Tiny particles suspended in the atmosphere.

Air mass   A large body of air with a uniform temperature and moisture content.

Air pollution   Any harmful substances introduced into the atmosphere.

Anoxic   An environment without oxygen.

Aquifer   Water stored in a groundwater system.

Atmosphere   One of the characteristic zones of Earth that includes the mixture of gases that surrounds the planet.

Basal sliding   Sliding of glacier ice due to reduced friction caused by water lubricating the surface under the glacier.

Base/basic   A substance with a pH higher than 7 due to an excess of hydroxide ions.

Bedrock   Solid rock underlying the soil.

Bioaccumulation   The buildup over time of toxins in a living organism.

Biochemical   Referring to chemical compounds that are part of biological organisms.

Biodegradable   A substance that can be broken down by biological processes into less toxic compounds.

Biogeochemical cycle   A cycling of some element through the environment due to biological, geological, and chemical actions.

Biological pathways   Chemical reactions that take place in living organisms.

Biomagnification   The concentration of toxins in an organism caused by eating other toxin-containing organisms.

Biomass   Organic matter found in the environment.

Biosphere   One of the characteristic zones of Earth that includes all living things.

Boiling point   The temperature at which a liquid becomes a gas.

Brine   Water with a large amount of dissolved salts.

Capillary action   The ability of water to rise in a thin tube due to cohesive and adhesive forces between the water and the material of the tube.

Cave   Any natural opening in the crust large enough to permit entry by humans.

Chemical weathering   The breaking down of rocks by chemical reactions that remove or dissolve minerals.

Chemosynthesis   The ability of some organisms to derive energy by breaking the bonds of chemical compounds.

Chlorofluorocarbon (CFC)   A class of mainly synthetic chemicals containing chlorine and fluorine bonded to carbon that are used in refrigeration and cooling.

Clastic   Sedimentary rocks formed from sediments that are cemented together, or lithified.

Cohesive forces   Forces between water molecules that hold the molecules together.

Cold front   The boundary formed when a cold air mass moves into a warmer air mass.

Colligative property   Properties such as freezing point and boiling point that are affected by the substances dissolved in a solvent.

Computer model   A mathematical representation describing the functions of a system that is run on a computer.

Condensation   A physical change of a gas to a liquid state.

Contaminants   Any substance that degrades the quality of air or water.

Continental crust   Rock that makes up the continents.

Convergent boundary   A zone where two tectonic plates are moving toward each other.

Core   The center of Earth.

Craton   The rocks the make up the oldest part of a continent.

Crust   The outer layer of the Earth.

Crystal   A lattice-like, ordered arrangement of atoms in a mineral.

Degradable   A substance that breaks down in the environment to form less toxic compounds.

Denitrification   The conversion of nitrogen compounds to nitrogen gas.

Density   The mass of a specific unit of volume of a material.

Deposition   Process by which sediments moved by agents of erosion are left in a new location.

Dissociate   The breaking of ionic bonds in substance.

Dissolution   Breaking ionic bonds in a compound by a polar solvent.

Divergent boundary   A zone where two tectonic plates are moving away from each other.

Erosion   The removal and transport of sediments by wind, water, or moving ice.

Evaporation   A physical change of a liquid to a gaseous state.

Exosphere   The outermost layer of the atmosphere.

Extrusive igneous rocks   Rocks formed from molten material at or near Earth's surface.

Fault   A weak zone in the crust along which the rocks crack and slide.

Food chain   A representation of how energy flows from the Sun, to plants, and finally to animals.

Forcings   Any factor that has a positive or negative affect on Earth's temperature.

Fossil fuels   Energy source that is based on carbon that was buried millions of years ago.

Frost wedging   The breaking or shattering of rock by repeated freezing and thawing of water.

Greenhouse effect   The warming effect caused by gases that trap heat in the atmosphere.

Greenhouse gas   Any gas that absorbs heat in the atmosphere.

Groundwater   Water found beneath Earth's surface in soil or rocks.

Heavy metals   Metals such as mercury, cadmium, arsenic, chromium, thallium, and lead that are found in the environment.

Humidity   The amount of water vapor in the atmosphere.

Hydrosphere   One of the characteristic zones of Earth that includes all the water.

Hypersaline   Water with more than the typical amount of dissolved salts.

Igneous rock   Rock formed from solidified molten material.

Infiltration   Water that enters the soil or rocks beneath the Earth's surface.

Intrusive igneous rocks   Rocks formed from molten material that solidified underground.

Ion exchange   Replacement of an ionic substance in a mineral by a different ionic substance with similar properties.

Isostatic rebound   The slow uplift of a region after the weight of continental ice has been removed.

Joint   A fracture in a rock along which no appreciable movement has occurred.

Lithify   The process by which sediments are compacted and turned into solid rock.

Lithosphere   One of the characteristic zones of Earth that includes the rocky surface.

Mantle   The middle layer of Earth.

Melting point   The temperature at which a solid becomes a liquid.

Mesosphere   Layer of the atmosphere where most meteors burn up.

Metamorphic rock   Rock formed from a different rock after it was exposed to high heat or pressure.

Mid-oceanic ridge   A ridge of igneous rocks that forms along a divergent boundary on the ocean floor.

Mineral   A naturally occurring chemical element or compound.

Nitrogen fixation   The conversion of atmospheric nitrogen to ammonia by bacteria.

Nonrenewable energy sources   Energy sources, such as fossil fuels, that are replenished at a much slower rate than they are used.

Occluded front   A condition where a cold front overtakes a warm front.

Oceanic crust   Rock that makes up the ocean floor.

Ore   A rock containing economically valuable minerals.

Orogen   The root of a mountain that extends deep into the crust.

Oxidation   A chemical reaction of a substance with oxygen.

Oxi-degradable   A substance that breaks down by oxidation into less toxic compounds.

Ozone   A form of oxygen composed of three oxygen atoms bonded together.

Particulate   A small particle of a liquid or solid that is suspended within a gas.

Pathogen   Disease-causing organism.

Permeability   A measure of open spaces in a rock.

Petroleum   Liquid organic compounds formed over long periods of time from ancient organic matter; also called oil.

pH   A measure of the hydronium ion concentration in a substance that determines whether the substance is acidic or basic.

Photolysis   A decomposition reaction caused by sunlight.

Physical weathering   The breaking of rocks through physical processes that cause cracking or shattering.

Plankton   Microscopic plants and animals living in the ocean.

Plastic flow   The ability of ice to behave like clay when exposed to high pressure.

Plate tectonics   The theory that explains how huge portions of Earth's lithosphere move slowly across Earth's surface.

Polymer   A long, chainlike molecule made up of repeating units.

Precipitation (chemical)   A chemical reaction that results in the formation of a solid.

Precipitation (weather)   Water or ice falling from clouds.

Regolith   A loose layer of broken rock and mineral fragments that covers much of Earth's land surface.

Relative humidity   A measure of the amount of water vapor in the air compared to the amount the air could hold at a given temperature.

Remediation   The process of cleaning up contaminants in the environment.

Renewable energy sources   Energy sources, such as wind and solar, that are continually replenished.

Rift   A wide valley formed at a divergent boundary.

Rock cycle   A cycle through which rocks change between being igneous, sedimentary, or metamorphic.

Rock flour   Rock ground to a very fine powder by glaciers.

Runoff   Water that flows across the Earth's surface after precipitation occurs.

Salinity   A measure of the amount of salts dissolved in water.

Sedimentary rock   Rock formed from debris, rocks, or sediments that were deposited and cemented together, or lithified.

Sediments   Rocks, sand, or debris deposited by wind, water, or chemical action.

Shield   The rock that makes up the oldest part of a continent.

Smog   A haze that forms from smoke and fog.

Smoke   Gases and particulates that result from combustion.

Soil   Rock fragments and organic matter that form a medium for plant growth; the uppermost layer of regolith, it can support rooted plants.

Solvent   The largest component of a solution.

Specific gravity   The ratio of the mass of a substance when compared to an equal volume of water.

Specific heat capacity   The ability of a substance to hold heat.

Stationary front   The boundary formed where a warm air mass and a cold air mass meet and stall.

Stratosphere   Layer of the atmosphere where the ozone layer is found.

Subduction zone   Zone where convergent tectonic plates come together and one plate dives under another.

Surface tension   The force formed by molecules at the surface of a liquid.

System   A group of interactions that fit together and can be isolated from other independently functioning groups.

Transform boundaries   A zone where two tectonic plates are sliding past each other.

Transpiration   The release of water vapor through the leaves of plants.

Troposphere   The lowest level of the atmosphere, where most weather occurs.

Vapor pressure   The pressure exerted by a liquid as it evaporates.

Vog   A haze that forms from volcanic emission of sulfur dioxide and fog.

Warm front   The boundary of a warm air mass that is moving into cooler air.

Water cycle   A cycle that describes how water moves through the hydrosphere, atmospheres, lithosphere, and biosphere.

Water vapor   The gaseous form of water.

Weathering   The breakdown of material caused by direct contact with the Earth's atmosphere.

BIBLIOGRAPHY

Banquieri, Eduardo. *The Biosphere (Our Planet)*. New York: Chelsea House Publications, 2005.

Cotton, William R. *Human Impacts on Weather and Climate*. New York: Cambridge University Press, 2007.

Henson, Robert. *The Rough Guide to Weather*. London, UK: Rough Guides, 2007.

Linden, Eugene. *The Winds of Change : Climate, Weather, and the Destruction of Civilizations*. New York: Simon & Schuster, 2006.

Martin, Walter E. and Nelson Nunnally. *Air and Water: An Introduction to the Atmosphere and the Hydrosphere*. Dubuque, IA: Kendall/Hunt Publishing Company, 2003.

Mathez, Edmond A. *The Earth Machine: The Science of a Dynamic Planet*. New York: Columbia University Press, 2004.

Reynolds, Ross. *Cambridge Guide to the Weather*. New York: Cambrige University Press, 2000.

Singh, R. B. *Ecological Techniques and Approaches to Vulnerable Environment: Hydrosphere-Geosphere Interaction*. Enfield, NH: Science Publishers, 1998.

Smil,Vaclav. *The Earth's Biosphere: Evolution, Dynamics, and Change*. Cambridge, MA: The MIT Press, 2003.

Stevens, William K. *The Change in the Weather : People, Weather, and the Science of Climate*. New York: Dell Publishing, 2001.

Stüwe, Kurt. *Geodynamics of the Lithosphere: An Introduction*. New York: Springer, 2007.

FURTHER READING

Cullen, Katherine E. *Weather and Climate : The People Behind the Science.* New York: Facts on File, 2006.

Desonie, Dana. *Hydrosphere.* Our Fragile Planet. New York: Chelsea House Publications, 2008.

Edwards, Dee, and Chris King, eds. *Geoscience: Understanding Geological Processes.* London: Hodder Murray, 1999.

Edwards, Katie and Brian Rosen. *From the Beginning (Earth).* London, UK: The Natural History Museum, 1999.

Vogt, Gregory. *The Biosphere: Realm of Life (Earth's Spheres).* Breckenridge, CO: Twenty-First Century Books, 2006.

Vogt, Gregory. *The Hydrosphere: Agent of Change (Earth's Spheres).* Breckenridge, CO: Twenty-First Century Books, 2006.

Vogt, Gregory. *The Lithosphere: Earth's Crust (Earth's Spheres).* Breckenridge, CO: Twenty-First Century Books, 2007.

Web Sites

National Oceanic and Atmospheric Administration
1401 Constitution Avenue, NW
Room 6217
Washington, DC 20230
Phone: (202) 482–6090
Fax: (202) 482–3154

http://www.noaa.gov/

United States Geological Survey
12201 Sunrise Valley Drive
Reston, VA 20192, USA
Phone: 703–648–4000

http://www.usgs.gov/

PHOTO CREDITS

INDEX

A

abrasion, 76
absolute humidity, 17
acid rain, 40–41, 51, 61, 76
acidic water, 50–51
adhesive forces, 46–47
aerosols, 17–18, 40
air masses, 24–25
air pollution, 37, 39
air pressure, 18–20
algae, 64
alkanes, 90–91
aluminum, 71
amethyst, 82
ammonia, 22, 23, 69, 100
animal respiration, 24, 29–30,
    93, 98
anoxic environment, 23, 64
Antarctic air masses, 25
Antarctica, ozone hole over, 38
anthracite, 91
aquifers, 55, 56–57
Arctic air masses, 25
argon, 15
Arrhenius, Svante, 32–33
arsenic, 51
asthenosphere, 68
atmosphere, 1, 15–28
    absorption of heat by, 30–35
    carbon dioxide in, 2, 15, 17,
        22–24, 103
    chemical processes in, 29–41
    composition of, 2, 15–18
    greenhouse gases in, 17, 30–31,
        32, 34
    hydrosphere and, 92
    life and, 29–30
    origin and evolution of,
        22–24
    oxygen in, 2, 3, 15, 22–24, 70
    ozone in, 15, 35–39
    protection of the, 41
    sulfur dioxide in, 39–41
    thickness and pressure of,
        18–20
    weather and, 24–28
atmospheric layers, 20–22
atmospheric pressure, 18–20

B

bacteria
    cyanobacteria, 22–23
    E. coli, 62
    nitrogen-fixing, 100
barometer, 18–19
barometric pressure, 18–20
Barrell, Joseph, 68
basal sliding, 57
basalt, 6, 11
basic water, 50–51
bedrock, 73, 75
bicarbonate ions, 78
bioaccumulation, 95–97
biochemical products, 6
biodegradable, 63
biogeochemical cycles, 97–102
    carbon cycle, 98–100
    nitrogen cycle, 30, 100–102
    phosphorus cycle, 101–102
    water cycle, 49, 56, 70, 305
biological pathways, 51
biomagnification, 96–97
biomass, 23
biosphere, 1, 93–105
    biogeochemical cycles, 97–102
    defined, 3, 93
    energy sources, 102–105
    food chains, 93–95
bituminous coal, 91–92
boiling point of water, 19, 47
breakage pattern, 87
brine, 52

C

cadmium, 51
calcite, 76
calcium, 49, 71
calcium carbonate, 6, 23, 50, 56, 79,
    87–88
calcium ions, 45
capillary action, 47
carbon, 3, 97
carbon cycle, 98–100
carbon dioxide
    in atmosphere, 2, 15, 17, 22–24,
        103
    dissolution of, 78

carbon dioxide *(continued)*
   dissolved in oceans, 100
   as greenhouse gas, 31, 34
   plants and, 30
   released from fossil fuel combus-
     tion, 33, 92, 102–103
   rising levels of, 32–33
carbonate ions, 78
carbonate precipitation, 6, 93
carbonates, 89
carbonic acid, 78–79
caves, 77–79
cellular respiration, 98
chemical weathering, 24, 48, 75–79
chemosynthesis, 69
chloride ions, 43, 48, 52
chlorine, 37–39
chlorofluorocarbons (CFCs), 31,
   37–39
chromium, 51
Clarke, Frank Wigglesworth,
   70–71
clastic sediments, 6
Clean Air Act, 39
cleavage, 87
climate, 60. *See also* temperature;
   weather
climate change, 24, 32–35, 59, 103.
   See also greenhouse gases
clouds
   formation of, 4, 26–28
   precipitation and, 25, 28
   water vapor and, 1, 4
coal, 33, 91–92, 103
cohesive forces, 46
cold fronts, 25
colligative property, 54
color, 85
computer models, 35
condensation, 4
condensation nuclei, 26–27
contaminants, 61–66
contaminated soil, 64
continental air masses, 25
continental crust, 11, 69, 72
continental drift, 3, 68
convergent boundaries, 12–14
cooking, at high altitude, 19
coral reefs, 2

core, 10
Coriolis effect, 53, 54
covalent-bonded crystals, 84
cratons, 72
crude oil. *See* petroleum
crust
   composition of, 5, 10–11, 70–71
   continental, 11, 69, 72
   formation of, 69
   oceanic, 11, 69, 72–73
crystalline structures, 81, 82
crystals, 6, 81, 82, 84
currents, 53, 54
cyanobacteria, 22–23

D
DDT, 96
Dead Sea, 52
decomposition, 98–99
degradable processes, 63
denitrification, 101
density of water, 47
deposition, 7–9, 77–79
dissociate, 48
dissolution, 76, 77
divergent boundaries, 12, 13, 14
dolomite, 76
drinking water, 49, 51, 55
dust, 17

E
E. coli, 62
Earth. *See also specific systems*
   crust, 5, 10–11, 69–73
   features of, 1–2
   formation of, 69
   plate tectonics, 11–14
   structure of, 10–11
   systems, 1–3, 14
   warming, 30–41
   water on, 42–43
earthquakes, 12, 14
effervescence, 87–88
Einstein, Albert, 104
El Niño, 59–60
electrons, free, 21–22
energy
   nuclear, 104–105
   solar, 20, 30, 31

thermal, 17
    transfer of, in food chain, 93–95
energy sources, 102–105
erosion, 7–9, 57–58
evaporation, 3–4, 5
exosphere, 22
extrusive igneous rocks, 6
Exxon Valdez, 65

F
faults, 12
fecal coliform bacteria, 62
fertilizers, 61, 63–64
first atmosphere, 22
fish, 59–60, 64
food chain
    bioaccumulation in, 95–97
    biomagnification in, 96–97
    workings of, 93–95
forcings, 34–35
fossil fuels
    burning of, 17, 24, 33–34, 41, 92,
        102–103
    coal, 33, 91–92, 103
    creation of, 23
    dependence on, 102
    formation of, 33, 90–92, 99–100
    natural gas, 33, 91, 92
    petroleum, 33, 64–66, 90–92, 103
freeze-thaw cycles, 75–76
freezing point of water, 53–54
freshwater, properties of, 48–51
friction, 76
fronts, 25
frost wedging, 76
fuels, 91

G
gemstones, 81–82
geochemistry, 70–71
glaciers, 57–59, 76
global climate, 60. *See also* weather
global warming, 24, 32–35, 59, 103.
    See also greenhouse gases
gold, 81
Grand Canyon, 9
granite, 11, 81
gravity, 7, 18
Great Barrier Reef, 2

Great Salt Lake, 52
greenhouse effect, 17, 31–35
greenhouse gases, 17, 30–32, 34. *See
    also* carbon dioxide
groundwater, 5, 49, 55–57, 66–67
gypsum, 77

H
halides, 89
halite, 88
hard water, 49, 50
hardness
    of minerals, 86–87
    of water, 49–50
heat, water and, 47
heavy metals, 51
helium, 22
hemoglobin, 51
high altitudes, cooking at, 19
humans, 102
humidity, 17
humus, 73, 75
hydrocarbons, 37, 90–91
hydrochloric acid, 87–88
hydrogen, 22, 37, 97
hydrogen ions, 77
hydrogen sulfide, 30, 69
hydrologic cycle, 3–5, 49, 56, 70
hydrosphere, 1, 42–54. *See also* water
    components of, 2, 42
    lithosphere and, 92
    mass of, 42
    origin and evolution of, 44–45
    processes in, 54, 55–67
    water properties, 45–54
hypersalinity, 52

I
ice, 42, 45
    erosion and, 7
    glaciers, 57–59
    properties of, 47–48
    sea, 54
ice ages, 69–70
ice crystals, 26–27
igneous rocks, 5–6, 7
Industrial Revolution, 33, 103
infiltration, 4–5
inner core, 10

intrusive igneous rocks, 6
ion exchange, 76–77
ionic particles, 21–22
ionic-bonded crystals, 84
ionosphere, 21–22
ions, 48
iron, 3, 10, 51, 71
iron oxide, 23
isostatic rebound, 58–59

J
joints, 75

K
kerogen, 91

L
La Niña, 59–60
lakes, 49
lava, 6
lead, 51
limestone, 6, 7, 23, 56, 77–79, 100
limonite, 77
lithified, 6
lithosphere, 1, 68–79. *See also*
   minerals
   atmosphere and, 92
   chemical composition of, 70–73
   chemical processes in, 79, 80–92
   composition of, 2–3, 68–69
   hydrosphere and, 92
   origin and evolution of, 69–70
   structure of, 10–11
   tectonic plates, 12–14, 68
   types of rocks, 5–7
   weathering, 73–79
living organisms. *See also* biosphere
   atmosphere and, 29–30
   bioaccumulation in, 95–97
   carbon cycle and, 3
   chemical reactions of, 93–94
   evolution of, 23–24
   first, 69, 93
luster, 84–85

M
magma, 6, 12, 14
magnesium, 3, 49, 71
magnetic field, 10

magnetism, 88
mantle, 10
marble, 7
maritime air masses, 25
mass
   of atmosphere, 18
   of glaciers, 58
   of hydrosphere, 42
mass extinctions, 24
matter
   conversion of, to energy, 104
   transfer of, in food chain, 93–95
melting point, 47
meniscus, 47
mercaptan, 91
mercury, 51, 95
mercury barometer, 18–19
mesosphere, 20
metallic luster, 84
metals, 84
metamorphic rock, 6–7
methane, 15, 31, 34, 91
mid-oceanic ridges, 14, 72, 73
minerals
   chemical weathering of, 76–77
   composition and structure of,
      80–84, 88
   defined, 5, 81
   dissolution of, 76, 77
   formation of, 80, 81–84
   identification of, 84
   impurities in, 82
   physical properties of, 84–88
   rock-forming, 88–90
   in water, 49–51
mining, 61
Moh's Hardness Scale, 86
mountains, 2, 3, 12
muscovite mica, 81

N
Naica Mine, 83
native elements, 90
natural gas, 33, 91, 92
nickel, 10
nitrate ions, 100
nitric oxide, 100
nitrite ions, 100
nitrogen, 2, 15, 23, 24, 37, 97

nitrogen cycle, 30, 100–102
nitrogen dioxide, 41, 61, 100
nitrogen fixation, 100
nitrogen oxides, 37
nitrous oxide, 15, 31, 101
non-metallic luster, 84–85
nonrenewable energy sources, 103,
    104
nuclear energy, 104–105
nuclear fission, 104–105
nuclear reactors, 104

O
occluded fronts, 25
ocean water, 42–45, 51–54
oceanic crust, 11, 69, 72–73
oceans, 1
    carbon dioxide in, 100
    currents, 53, 54
    depths of, 43–44
    pollutants in, 63
    size of, 42–43
oil, 64–66
oil spills, 64–66
organic debris, 62
orogens, 72
outer core, 10
oxidants, 66, 67
oxidation, 77
oxi-degradable processes, 63
oxides, 23, 70, 71, 89–90
oxygen
    in atmosphere, 2, 3, 15, 22–24, 70
    in biogeochemical cycles, 97
    living organisms and, 29–30
    pollutants reacting with, 64
ozone
    in atmosphere, 15, 24, 35–39
    formation of, 35, 36, 37
    good and bad, 35, 37
    as greenhouse gas, 31, 37
ozone depletion, 37–39
ozone hole, 38
ozone layer, 2, 20, 24, 35, 37, 70

P
pathogens, 62
permeability, 4
pesticides, 61, 95–96

petroleum, 33, 64–66, 90–92, 103.
    See also fossil fuels
petroleum products, 61
pH, 50–51
phosphate salts, 101
phosphates, 90
phosphorous, 97
phosphorus cycle, 101–102
photolysis, 23
photosynthesis, 70, 93–94, 98
physical weathering, 75–76
plankton, 59–60
plant roots, 76
plants, 5, 30
plastic flow, 57, 63
plate boundaries, 12–14
plate tectonics, 11–14
polar air masses, 25
polarity, 45–46
pollutants
    chemical reactions of, 63–64
    identifying source of, 66
    types of, 61–63
pollution
    air, 37, 39
    water, 60–67
polymers, 63
potassium, 71
precipitation
    acid, 40–41, 51, 61, 76
    carbonate, 6, 93
    formation of, 25
    water cycle and, 4, 28, 49
pressure cookers, 19
primary producers, 94
protoplanets, 69
pyrolusite, 77

Q
quartz, 82

R
Radiation Budget, 30
radio waves, 22
radioactive waste, 105
rain, 28. *See also* precipitation
rain showers, 25
regolith, 73
relative humidity, 17

remediation, 66–67
renewable energy sources, 103–104
respiration, 24, 29–30, 93, 98
rifts, 14
rivers, 49, 63, 66
rock cycle, 7, 8
rock flour, 58
rock-forming minerals, 88–90
rocks
    igneous, 5–6, 7
    metamorphic, 6–7
    minerals and, 81
    sedimentary, 6, 7
    types of, 5–7
    weathering of, 75–76
rose quartz, 82
runoff, 4–5

S
salts, 48, 51–54
saltwater, 42–45, 51–54
San Andreas Fault, 14
sandstone, 56
scale, 50
sea ice, 54
sea salt, 52–53
seawater, 42–45, 51–54
second atmosphere, 22–24
sedimentary rock, 6, 7
sediments, 6
seismic waves, 10
selenite, 83
shale, 7
shells, 45
shields, 72
showers, 25
silicates, 88–89
silicon, 3, 71
silver, 81
skin cancer, 35
slate, 7
sleet, 28
smell, of minerals, 88
smog, 37, 39
smoke, 39
snow, 28
sodium, 71
sodium chloride, 48, 52, 88

sodium ions, 43, 45, 48, 52
soft water, 49
soil, 64, 73–75
soil permeability, 4
soil profile, 74
solar energy, 30, 31
solar heating, 20
solar system, 69
solutional processes, 77–79
solvent, 48
soot, 39
specific gravity, 68, 87
specific heat capacity, 47
springs, 49
stalactites, 78, 79
stalagmites, 78
stationary fronts, 25
steam, 22
stratosphere, 2, 20
streak, 85
streams, 49
subduction zones, 72, 73
subsoil, 74
substratum, 74
sucrose, 48
sulfates, 89
sulfides, 90
sulfur, 88, 97
sulfur dioxide, 39–41, 61
sulfuric acid, 40–41
Sun, 69
sunlight, 30, 69–70
surface horizon, 74
surface tension, 46
systems. *See also specific systems*
    defined, 1
    Earth, 1–3, 14

T
taste, of minerals, 88
tectonic plates, 12–14, 68
temperature
    changes of, in levels of
      atmosphere, 20–22
    on Earth, 2
    greenhouse effect and, 31–35
    water and, 47
    water vapor and, 17

thallium, 51
thermal energy, 17
thermosphere, 21–22
third atmosphere, 24
thunderstorms, 25
till, 57
titanium, 82
toxic chemicals, 61
trace gases, 30–31
transform boundaries, 13, 14
transpiration, 5
troposphere, 2, 20, 35, 37

U
ultraviolet radiation, 2, 20, 35,
     37, 70
uranium, 104
uranium-235, 104–105

V
Van der Waals forces, 84
Vernadsky, Vladimir, 93
vog, 39
volcanic eruptions, 39–40, 69
volcanoes, 12, 22

W
warm fronts, 25
water. *See also* ice
     abundance of, on Earth, 1–2,
          42–43
     acidic, 50–51
     basic, 50–51
     boiling point, 19, 47
     chemical formula, 45
     density of, 47
     drinking, 49, 51, 55
     erosion by, 7
     forms of, 2, 4
     freeze-thaw cycles, 75–76
     freezing point of, 53–54
     freshwater, 48–51
     gaseous, 42

groundwater, 5, 49, 55–57, 66–67
     hardness of, 49–50
     heat and, 47
     liquid, 30, 42
     melting point, 47
     molecular structure of, 45–46
     ocean, 42–45, 51–54
     pH of, 50–51
     properties of, 45–54
     soft, 49
     solid, 42
     as solvent, 48, 56
     source of, 44–45
     states of, 47–48
water cycle, 3–5, 49, 56, 70
water droplets, 26–27, 28
water pollution, 60–67
     chemical reactions of pollutants,
          63–64
     cleaning up, 66–67
     oil and petroleum, 64–66
     sources of, 61–63
water vapor
     in atmosphere, 1, 2, 15, 16–17, 42
     cloud formation and, 26–28
     experiment, 27
     as greenhouse gas, 31
     properties of, 45
     water cycle and, 3–4
weather, 24–28
     air masses, 24–25
     clouds and precipitation, 26–28
     El Niño, 59–60
     fronts, 25
     La Niña, 59–60
     in troposphere, 20
weathering
     chemical, 75–79
     defined, 7, 73
     physical, 75–76
     soil formation by, 73–75
     zone, 73
wind, 7

ABOUT THE AUTHOR

ALLAN B. COBB is a science writer who lives in central Texas. Before becoming a writer, he worked as a biologist, chemist, and environmental scientist. When not writing about science, he enjoys exploring nature. He travels in Central America to work with archeological projects as a science specialist. He enjoys exploring deserts, mountains, jungles, and beaches. His travels and hobbies give him a special insight into the workings of Earth.